SoJourn
Volume 1, Number 2

A journal devoted to the history, culture, and geography of South Jersey

Winter 2016/17

SoJourn is a collaborative effort. Local historians contribute the articles; Stockton students—in this issue, the editing interns of fall 2016—edit the articles, set the type and design the layout; the directors of the South Jersey Culture & History Center at Stockton University oversee the publication.

Editors
Maria K. Armstrong, Dominique A. DeFilippis, Kristen DeLeonard, Brielle Elise, Lindsay S. Ferrigno, James Gordon, Erin K. O'Leary, Nicolette T. Olivieri, Brian T. Stolz, Alison L. Todd, Nolan R. Wentworth.

Editors in chief
Tom Kinsella and Paul W. Schopp

ISSN: 2474-6665

ISBN: 978-0-9976699-2-3

A publication of the South Jersey Culture & History Center
at Stockton University
blogs.stockton.edu/sjchc/

© 2017, the authors, South Jersey Culture & History Center, and Stockton University. All rights reserved.

Filler images, at the conclusion of articles, courtesy of the Paul W. Schopp Collection.

To contact SJCHC write:
SJCHC
School of Arts & Humanities
Stockton University
101 Vera King Farris Drive
Galloway, New Jersey
08205

Email:
Thomas.Kinsella@stockton.edu

About this Issue of *SoJourn*

The goal of *SoJourn* is twofold: to inform and entertain. The subject matter varies in location and time, with the only requirement that it relate to the rich history and culture of the eight southernmost counties of New Jersey: *South Jersey*. This second issue reaches back to the eighteenth century, albeit through discussion of a mid-nineteenth-century novel, and stretches forward to the summer of 2016, describing a day spent with a Leeds Point crabber. Essays touch upon local industries—sawmills, fishing, crabbing and fruitpicking—upon art—architecture, literature and, again, fruitpicking—and also upon notable citizens—Margaret Mead, the Rev. Jeremiah H. Pierce, and four generations of Butcher MDs. This brief listing supplies little insight into the breadth of the articles here. Neither does it suggest the matrix of ideas that interweave and connect the varied subjects. For that, dear readers, you will have to search for yourselves. If you do, we trust that you will enjoy the experience.

> Tom Kinsella
> Director, South Jersey Culture & History Center
> Stockton University

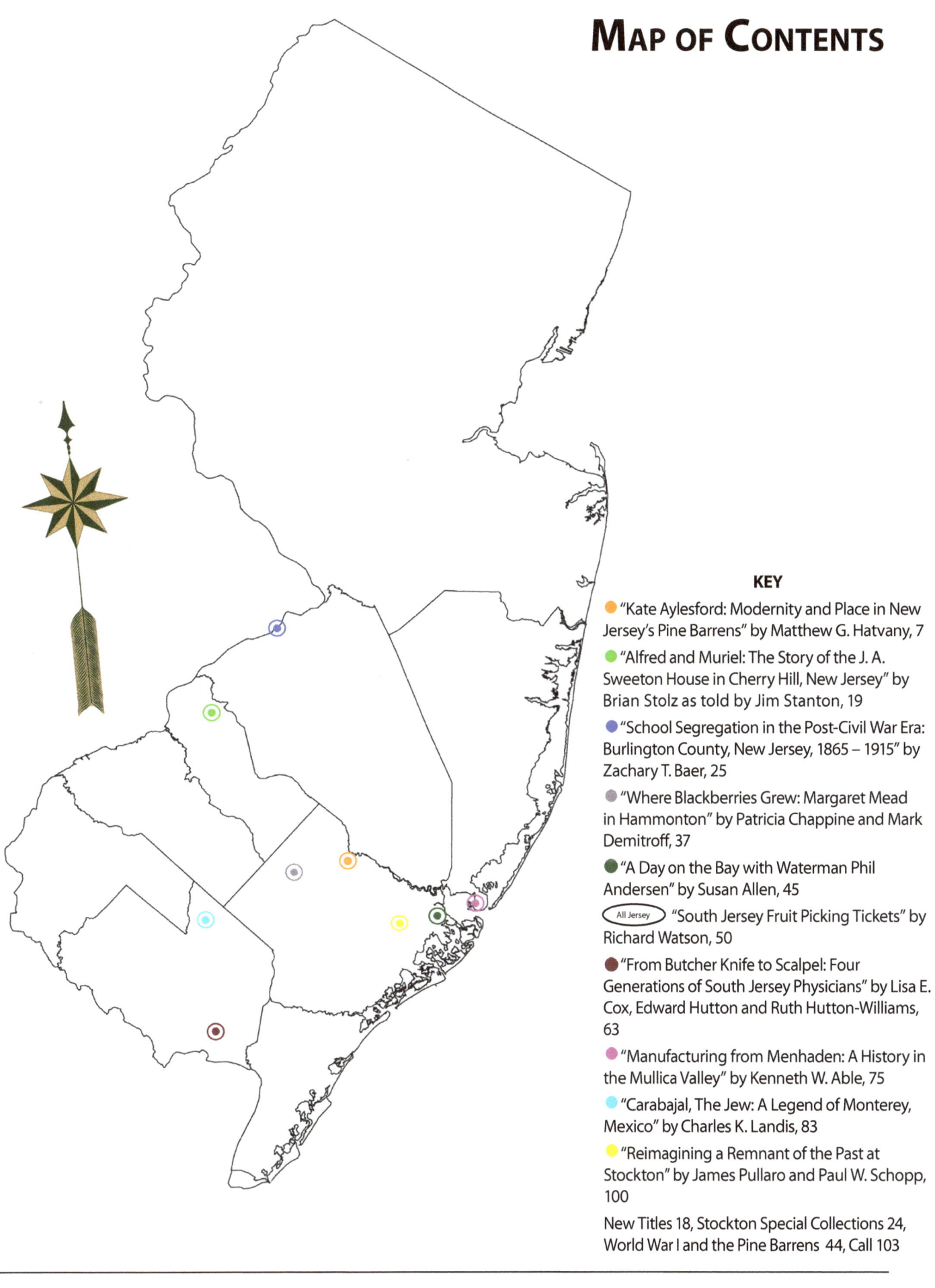

Map of Contents

KEY

- 🟠 "Kate Aylesford: Modernity and Place in New Jersey's Pine Barrens" by Matthew G. Hatvany, 7
- 🟢 "Alfred and Muriel: The Story of the J. A. Sweeton House in Cherry Hill, New Jersey" by Brian Stolz as told by Jim Stanton, 19
- 🔵 "School Segregation in the Post-Civil War Era: Burlington County, New Jersey, 1865 – 1915" by Zachary T. Baer, 25
- 🟣 "Where Blackberries Grew: Margaret Mead in Hammonton" by Patricia Chappine and Mark Demitroff, 37
- 🟢 "A Day on the Bay with Waterman Phil Andersen" by Susan Allen, 45
- (All Jersey) "South Jersey Fruit Picking Tickets" by Richard Watson, 50
- 🟤 "From Butcher Knife to Scalpel: Four Generations of South Jersey Physicians" by Lisa E. Cox, Edward Hutton and Ruth Hutton-Williams, 63
- 🩷 "Manufacturing from Menhaden: A History in the Mullica Valley" by Kenneth W. Able, 75
- 🩵 "Carabajal, The Jew: A Legend of Monterey, Mexico" by Charles K. Landis, 83
- 🟡 "Reimagining a Remnant of the Past at Stockton" by James Pullaro and Paul W. Schopp, 100

New Titles 18, Stockton Special Collections 24, World War I and the Pine Barrens 44, Call 103

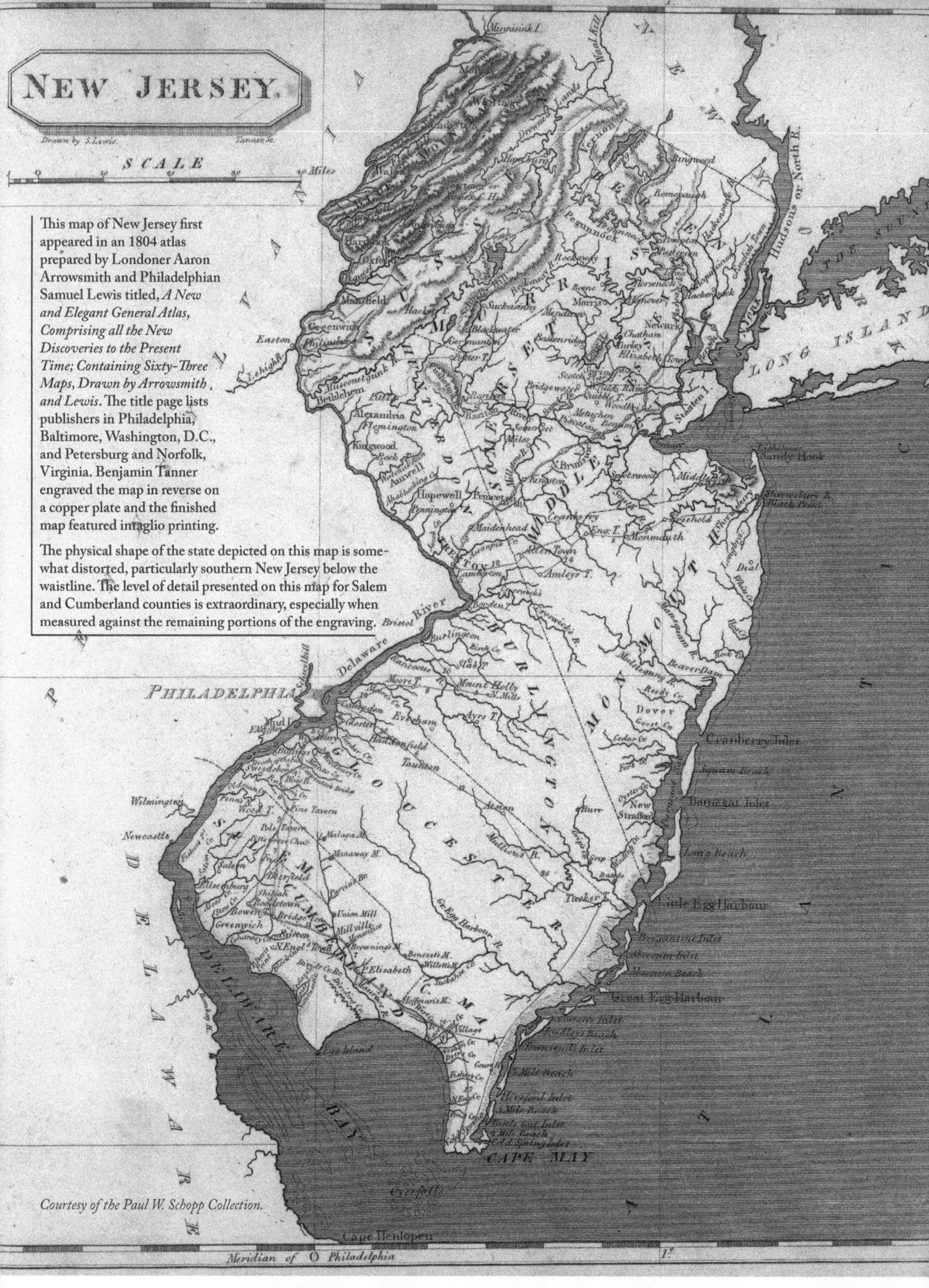

NEW JERSEY.

Drawn by S. Lewis. *Tanner Sc.*

This map of New Jersey first appeared in an 1804 atlas prepared by Londoner Aaron Arrowsmith and Philadelphian Samuel Lewis titled, *A New and Elegant General Atlas, Comprising all the New Discoveries to the Present Time; Containing Sixty-Three Maps, Drawn by Arrowsmith and Lewis.* The title page lists publishers in Philadelphia, Baltimore, Washington, D.C., and Petersburg and Norfolk, Virginia. Benjamin Tanner engraved the map in reverse on a copper plate and the finished map featured intaglio printing.

The physical shape of the state depicted on this map is somewhat distorted, particularly southern New Jersey below the waistline. The level of detail presented on this map for Salem and Cumberland counties is extraordinary, especially when measured against the remaining portions of the engraving.

Courtesy of the Paul W. Schopp Collection.

Kate Aylesford
Modernity and Place in New Jersey's Pine Barrens

Matthew G. Hatvany

As anyone who has read John McPhee's *The Pine Barrens* (1967) can attest, when it comes to the opposing dualities of "place" and "placelessness," the Pine Barrens region was, and continues to be, the antithesis of metropolitan New Jersey. In the last century and a half, New Jersey has increasingly become a mosaic of anonymous suburbs in one of the most densely populated and industrial states in the Union—a historical progression in stark opposition to that of the Pine Barrens region. In the Colonial and Early Republic periods, the Pine Barrens formed an almost uninterrupted swath of pine and oak forests, extending from Cape May County to Middlesex County along the Outer Coastal Plain, interspersed with numerous cedar swamps.

The region offered to successive waves of exploiters a wide variety of natural resources from which to gain profits, starting with cedar and other timber, charcoal production, and mill seats, primarily for sawmills. The discovery of bog iron provided the Pines Barrens with a new economic engine. Nearly thirty iron furnace and forge communities sprang up, which combined to make the Pines one of the industrial centers in North America. Yet, by 1850, while modernity brought rapid industrial development to the Eastern Seaboard, the Pine Barrens had lapsed into relative decline, marked by deindustrialization, depopulation, re-naturalization, and a heightened sense of "place" for those who chose to remain behind.[1] It is difficult to imagine that the mainly forested Pinelands National Reserve of today—some 1.1 million acres in area—had, in the eighteenth and early nineteenth centuries, been a leading place of commerce and industry.[2]

Fifty years ago, local historian Harriet S. Sander wrote of modernity arriving in the Pine Barrens village of Port Republic:

> The town is crossed and criss-crossed by roads, modern, well paved, well kept and patrolled. But these roads have felt the tread of moccasined feet, the heavy tread of Continental boots.... But somehow along the way they lost their identity and became modern."[3]

"Identity" and "modern" are two recurring words that seem inseparable when discussing contemporary New Jersey, and not necessarily for their complementarity. Rather, many invoke the concept of modernity in

The Kate Aylesford Mansion, Pleasant Mills, New Jersey, built for Elijah Clark, c.1760. *Courtesy of the Paul W. Schopp Collection.*

opposition to a "perceived" loss of the "sense of place" in industrial and post-industrial New Jersey.[4] Situated today between the first and fifth largest cities in America, New Jersey developed as a hinterland of New York and Philadelphia. Unable to develop a metropolis rivaling those cities, New Jersey has historically been subject to externally based metropolitan views portraying the state as essentially "placeless"—a transportation corridor between its two dominant neighbors.[5]

While metropolitan pundits have had difficulty pinpointing a distinctively "Jersey" sense of place, that very theme dominates the pages of Charles Jacobs Peterson's *Kate Aylesford: A Story of the Refugees* (1855), one of New Jersey's earliest historical romance novels set in the Pine Barrens.[6] Literature specialists consider the author of this novel, out of print for nearly a century and a half, a mediocre "magazinist and pulp writer of the middle of the nineteenth century."[7] Few copies of the original book survive, but as Robert Bateman, the scholar instrumental in its republication in 2001, comments in the foreword to the new edition, it is "a touchstone of sorts, a book that once read will reveal a long-dead past ripe with worthwhile information and entertaining incidents. For others, it remains an obscure and mislabeled oddity, a novel usually mentioned in passing but never actually examined."[8]

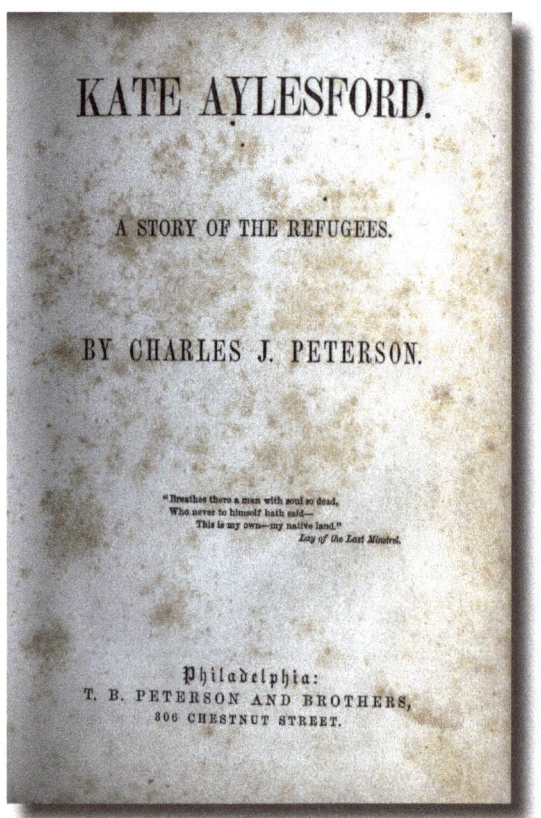

Title page of *Kate Aylesford*, first edition. *Courtesy of the Paul W. Schopp Collection.*

A Geo-Historical Consideration

The better-known authors and historians of the Pine Barrens—Henry Charlton Beck, Arthur Pierce, and John McPhee—found the story and characters behind Peterson's book intriguing. Nonetheless, they never considered it beyond its nostalgic value. Robert Bateman, however, argues that the book deserves more credit as an early example of Mid-Atlantic (New York, New Jersey, Pennsylvania, Delaware, and Maryland) historical romance. Its neglect likely stems from the overwhelming emphasis in early American literature upon antebellum New England and Southern texts.[9] Another contributing factor, as Barrie Hayne points out, is the lack of attention given to the author and even less to his connections with the Pine Barrens.[10] While Peterson was a prolific writer and editor of magazines, he left behind few direct clues regarding the origins and inspiration of *Kate Aylesford*.[11]

Because Peterson's prose falls short when compared to his more famous contemporaries from the Mid-Atlantic, like Walt Whitman and Edgar Allan Poe, it has precluded critics from appreciating the important manner in which *Kate Aylesford* elucidates concepts of "place" and "placelessness" at a critical juncture in American history and literature. Modernity, in the form of theodolites, railroads, capitalist industrial relations, land speculation, urbanization, and mass immigration, was rapidly transforming traditional socio-economic ties to the land. Underlying the obvious commercial intentions of the novel, it can be argued that *Kate Aylesford* was not the musings of a mediocre writer plying the romantic susceptibilities of a nostalgia-hungry public. Rather, it is the work of a resourceful writer articulating and objectifying his passion for the land and people of his youth, and his very real unease over the deindustrialization of the Pine Barrens and the consequent re-ordering of the physical and cultural landscape.[12] In this light, Peterson is one of many mid-nineteenth-century Anglo-American writers who turned to the historical romance novel as a medium to express a profound personal interest in the influence of time and modernity on "place."

This study takes its inspiration from the well-known work of H. C. Darby, British historical geographer, on Thomas Hardy's fictional region of Wessex. In the pages of *Kate Aylesford*, it is possible to examine the geo-historical techniques Charles Jacobs Peterson used, which convey to readers the impact of modernity on the Pine Barrens. It was a modernity derived from seemingly uncontrollable economic and cultural changes that originated from outside the Pine Barrens and menaced the traditional relationship between people and land.[13]

Landscape and the Historical Romance Novel

Set in revolutionary New Jersey, *Kate Aylesford* was a well-received story that *Putnam's Monthly Magazine* acclaimed "a romantic but truthful story of the refugees of New Jersey, during the time of the Revolution, told with simplicity and earnestness, but with great dramatic effect. This kind of historical novel has gone out of date for the present, but Mr. Peterson has revived it with a rare knowledge of its capabilities."[14]

It is a story of love and war as experienced by a Tory sympathizer, Kate Aylesford of Sweetwater (today's Pleasant Mills), and a Philadelphia lawyer turned Patriot, Major Gordon, during the 1778 Battle of Chestnut Neck (near today's Port Republic), where American Patriots prevented British forces from ascending the Mullica River and burning the iron furnace at Batsto. While the developing romance between Kate and Major Gordon dominates the story, a continuous geo-historical narrative explores the opposing dualities of modernity and place just below the surface. Nature and culture, city and country, corruption and salvation, tradition and modernity, place and placelessness: all of these dualities are found in much of the subsequent literature on the Pine Barrens (table 1).

The historical romance novel, blending incidents of local history and geography with fictional plots, was much in evidence during the Victorian era.[15] Notable American examples of this genre include Washington Irving's treatment of the disappearing Dutch society in the Hudson Valley in *Rip Van Winkle* (1819); James Fenimore Cooper's tales of the clash of Native American and European cultures around Lake Champlain in the *Leatherstocking Tales* (1823 – 1841); Whitman's concern with the fading memory of the remaining Revolutionary soldiers in *The Last of the Sacred Army* (1840s); Hawthorne's *The Scarlet Letter* (1850), dealing with religious intolerance in New England; and Herman Melville's preoccupation with the human struggle to dominate nature in *Moby Dick* (1851). While it was a work of non-fiction, one might even include in this list Henry David Thoreau's *Walden* (1854) and his concern with documenting the disappearance of primal nature and intimate relations with the land in the face of rapid industrialization. This genre reached its apogee with Mark Twain's tales of life on the Mississippi in the late nineteenth century. While the writings of Peterson, a highly accomplished Philadelphia author, magazine publisher, and historian, have never been completely forgotten by regional specialists, it is only with the relatively recent reprinting of *Kate Aylesford* in 2001 that a renewed interest in the book has occurred.[16]

The Changing Landscape

In 1855, when 36-year-old Charles J. Peterson published *Kate Aylesford*, time and modernity were erasing many of the hallowed places of the Revolutionary heroes from the American landscape. The years immediately following Peterson's birth, in Philadelphia in 1819, witnessed the enormous physical, economic, demographic, and technological growth of the country, and, at the same time, the passing of the last of the nation's founders: Jefferson and Adams in 1826, Monroe in 1831, as well as the last remaining soldiers from what Whitman called "The Sacred Army."[17] By Peterson's twentieth birthday, the circles remaining from British tents on the Boston Common had all but disappeared. It is believed that Peterson spent the summers of his youth in Pleasant Mills, the "Sweetwater" of Kate Aylesford, listening to his grandfather, Lawrence Peterson, recount stories of his exploits at the battles of Trenton and Chestnut Neck.[18] At the same time, the young Peterson witnessed firsthand the rapid demise of the iron industry in the Pine Barrens and the consequent repurposing and platting of the vast tracts of charcoal-producing forest and ore-rich swamps. Rootedness in the Pine Barrens, as so many remarked across America in the 1840s and 1850s, was yielding to an accelerating rhythm of foreclosure, dispossession, and diaspora.[19]

Author	Title	Date	NF	F	Geo-Historical Narrative
C. J. Peterson	*Kate Aylesford*	1855		√	Nature/Culture, Modernity/Identity
W. F. Mayer	"In the Pines"	1859	√		Nature/Culture
H. C. Beck	*Jersey Genesis*	1945	√		Modernity/Identity
J. McPhee	*The Pine Barrens*	1967	√		Nature/Culture, Modernity/Identity
J. McPhee	"People of the P. Barrens"	1974	√		Nature/Culture, Modernity/Identity
R. Bateman	*Pinelands*	1994		√	Nature/Culture, Modernity/Identity

Table 1. Opposing dualities in notable fictional (F) and non-fictional (NF) Pine Barrens literature.[20]

That sense of "place"—the experiential combination of setting, environment, ritual and routine that give people emotional and spiritual bonds to the land—was eroding from the Pine Barrens landscape.[21] In *Kate Aylesford*, Peterson continually underscores this loss when he describes, for example, the battlefield at Chestnut Neck or the privateer haven on the Mullica River known as The Forks.

In September 1778, New Jersey Patriots erected breastworks at Chestnut Neck in an attempt to prevent British forces from ascending the river and sacking The Forks. The poorly trained militia troops failed to hold Chestnut Neck, and British forces sailed up the Mullica and burned The Forks. Yet the courage that the Patriots demonstrated, and the timely reinforcement by Count Casimir Pulaski and his cavalry, proved sufficient to check the British before they could reach the iron furnace at Batsto (Waldo Furnace in the novel).[22]

It is the facts and legends surrounding this story that Peterson uses to draw readers into what he deemed the "fast disappearing" landscape of the eighteenth-century Pine Barrens. Drawing on his intimate knowledge of the local geography, culture, and history of the region, Peterson related to his readers how The Forks had served as a privateer's haven. The village was, in Peterson's words,

Monument at Chestnut Neck, New Jersey, commemorating the battle. *Courtesy of the Paul W. Schopp Collection.*

> Situated at the head of navigation . . . It was a settlement comprising about twenty-five houses . . . the western shore of the narrow but deep river in front, was lined for a considerable distance with vessels . . . fat merchantmen . . . there contributing unwillingly to the wealth of American patriots; and many a proud West Indiaman, which had been freighted . . . for London, was now unloading for the benefit of Philadelphia.[23]

Nevertheless, as Peterson contemplated that hallowed site from his vantage point in 1855, nearly every vestige of the former village had disappeared, "except a solitary domicile, and a few grand old buttonwoods [trees]."[24] Other Pine Barrens authors would write with the same melancholy sense of loss resulting from modernity and the passage of time. In 1859, W. F. Mayer's article in *The Atlantic* provided details about Hanover furnace, one of the many isolated iron-producing villages dotting the late eighteenth- and early nineteenth-century landscape in the Pine Barrens:

> [In its day, Hanover] furnished many a city with its iron tubes for water and for gas, many a factory and workshop with its castings, many a farmer with his tools; but the glow of the furnace is quenched forever now. The slowly gathering ferruginous [iron] deposits have been exhausted, and three years have elapsed since the furnace-fires were lighted. The blackened shell of the building stands in cold decrepitude, a melancholy vestige of usefulness outlived. In consequence of the stoppage of the works, Hanover has lost seven-eighths of its population, and only about fifty inhabitants remain in the white cottages grouped about the Big House, who are employed in agricultural labors and occupations connected with the forest.[25]

Some thirty years later in 1885, state geologist C. Clarkson Vermeule wrote:

> From Manchester southward to the Mullica River is one of the wildest, most desolate portions of the State . . . not more than 2 percent of the area is under cultivation. Here and there are narrow roads, barely wide enough for a single vehicle to pass clear of the trees, which thread their lonely way from clearing to clearing. They are relics of a time when the manufacture of iron from bog ore found in the swamps was an important industry of the region. Here and there one comes upon abandoned forge sites, or still more suggestive, abandoned villages, the relics of unsuccessful glass manufacture in the wilderness. An indescribable silence prevails.[26]

Another thirty years later, in 1916, while the state of New Jersey was already well on its way to becoming a modern industrial powerhouse, John Harshberger, renowned Philadelphia botanist and Pine Barrens expert, wrote that the Pine Barrens region was now, "in many places an unbroken wilderness. The drainage area of the Wading River is one of the wildest, most desolate portions of the eastern United States, and the writer has traveled a distance of 16 kilometers (10 miles) without seeing a house or a human being."[27]

Peterson weaves his personal experience as a youth in the Pine Barrens into the pages of *Kate Aylesford* when he remarks that in the 1820s and 1830s, one could walk for "miles on miles by an almost unbroken forest"; the very atmosphere of the place, he continues, "breathes of peace and happiness."[28] Often, he whiles away the long and hot summer days at Pleasant Mills gazing down from a wooden dam spanning the river draining Lake Nescochague. He stood there motionless, he recalls, listening, "in a dreamy languor," to the gurgle of the tea-colored cedar waters race over the spillway.[29] As he walked those sandy pine-scented roads and observed the cedar waters coursing their way to the Mullica River, Peterson was a conscious witness to the collapse of the iron villages in the Pine Barrens; it is this fact that makes *Kate Aylesford* an important source for geo-historical analysis.

As an adolescent enjoying visits from Philadelphia to his paternal grandfather Lawrence's home at Pleasant Mills, Peterson unwittingly left traces of his personal connection with the Pine Barrens. His name appears in the Batsto store ledgers, interspaced among the names of the iron furnace workers: molders, colliers, core makers, and wagon teamsters.[30] Other traces of the Peterson name are evident on eight headstones in the cemetery of the Methodist Church at Pleasant Mills that Peterson's grandfather, one of the original Swedish settlers of the area, helped to establish in the late 1700s. Peterson fondly describes this locale in *Kate Aylesford*: "Beside the church is a grave-yard, surrounded by a rude fence, and shaded by oak trees. The birds build their nests undisturbed here, and the grass and wild flowers bloom and fade in peace."[31] Only a few minutes from this bucolic setting was the iron furnace at Batsto. In his youth, Peterson witnessed its demise as it slipped into a phase of deindustrialization over which the entire region had little control.

A Narrative of Opposing Forces

It was not only the physical landscape that underwent change as a result of modernity; it was equally the "sense of place." When Major Gordon first attends Sunday services at Sweetwater (Pleasant Mills), Peter-

The Batsto dam c. 1906 in Batsto Village, New Jersey. *Courtesy of the Paul W. Schopp Collection.*

son describes the major leaving church and observing the headstones in the cemetery:

> [Gordon turns] aside into the grave-yard, on the right of the church. It was a spot that might have been selected for an elegy.... There were few headstones in that humble cemetery; no pompous heraldic emblems; nothing of the usual vanities of life, that seem, in similar places, such a mockery of death. Good and true men, who, in their lowly walk, had lived more nobly than Pharaohs who now slumber beneath pyramids ... slept there unheralded, and forgotten by all, except by the descendants who still reverenced their virtues.[32]

The "descendants" to whom Peterson refers is himself. There in the graveyard, Major Gordon had his first opportunity to speak at length with Lawrence Herman, a descendant of the original Swedish settlers of the region. Peterson modeled Herman, many believe, on his grandfather, Lawrence Peterson. An elder in the community and a veteran of the Battle of Trenton, Herman is affectionately called "Uncle Lawrence" by Kate Aylesford. The historical parallels here with Peterson's own grandfather, who fought in the Battles of Trenton and Chestnut Neck, are obvious.[33] God-fearing, living off the fruits of his labor as a small freeholder who is intimately tied to the land and his modest home, Peterson portrays Uncle Lawrence as an American yeoman, "nature's nobleman," and Gordon quickly comes to depend on him for advice in the defense of Chestnut Neck. When the attack comes, Gordon calls for volunteers, and it is Uncle Lawrence who steps forward as a patriotic example to others. Through that action, Uncle Lawrence becomes the prototype of the Revolutionary Patriot, exuding a sense of brotherhood and inborn equality with his fellow Americans, even when, much later in the story, he finds himself face to face with General George Washington.

The author contrasts these qualities of the "Jeffersonian" yeoman in the Pine Barrens with that of Charles Aylesford, Kate's Tory cousin and Major Gordon's rival for her affections. Unlike Gordon, who appreciates the humble skills and God-fearing demeanor of Uncle Lawrence, Charles Aylesford holds him in disdain. Charles Aylesford, who hails from Philadelphia, spends his time and fortune following the fleeting urban fashions of the day. Having lost his wealth in the city, he returns to Sweetwater to win the hand of Kate. Far from a romantic, Charles means to seize the family estate for himself. Charles Aylesford was, Peterson notes, "like most fashionable profligates of that day, an atheist at heart. It was an age when the French Encylopaediastes had exhausted every resource of sophistry and satire to

The British-American Battlefield of Chestnut Neck, New Jersey. Photo by M. H. Kirscht. *Courtesy of the Paul W. Schopp Collection.*

shake the belief in divine revelation; when young men thought it smart to laugh at the Bible, as a collection of old legends only fit for women."³⁴

Readers are led to understand how the decadence of city life permitted Charles to secretly corrupt a young Philadelphian, Mary Rowan, and father a child out of wedlock. Back in Sweetwater, as the lines of battle are being drawn between British and Patriot forces at Chestnut Neck, Major Gordon gives his full attention to the impending skirmish. At that moment Charles kidnaps Kate in hopes of spiriting her behind British lines and forcing her to marry him. This plan goes awry when Patriot soldiers mortally wound him. Yet even in the throes of death, Charles Aylesford stubbornly refuses the redemption a clergyman offers him. This ignoble end contrasts with that of Uncle Lawrence, who, in the failed attempt to hold Chestnut Neck, becomes a prisoner, along with Major Gordon. They are surely to be led to a prison ship for the duration of the war. Unexpectedly, Captain Powell, a British officer whom Major Gordon saved from drowning at the beginning of the story, sets both men free. Powell asserts, "I owe you a heavy debt, and I have come to pay it, by setting you free." Upon hearing this, Uncle Lawrence acclaims, "The Lord's hand is in it.... Did I not say, 'trust in the Lord,' Major?"

Modernity, Sense of Place, and Placelessness

The story ends with the rescue of Kate and her subsequent marriage to Major Gordon at a grandiose wedding in Philadelphia. Gordon then returns to private life as a city lawyer. This passage from country to city symbolizes the actual youth of Peterson, who studied to become a Philadelphia lawyer. Mirroring Peterson's later life, Major Gordon and Kate Aylesford reside in the city, but return periodically to the Pine Barrens to refresh their connection with the land, nature, and their patriotic "benefactor," Uncle Lawrence. Yet, just as the last of the Patriots and physical relics of the Revolutionary War disappear from the Pine Barrens landscape, so too does Uncle Lawrence and his agrarian ways. With his death, Peterson laments that Uncle Lawrence's modest farm has passed,

> into other hands. Lately it has been abandoned to the forest, which is growing up, wild and rank, on the fields where the patriarch tilled the soil, and close around the hearth where he offered his morning and evening prayers. Mother earth has claimed not only his own ashes, but even "the place that knew him."³⁵

Uncle Lawrence's passing symbolizes the waning of the traditional Pine Barrens landscape that, with the coming of modernity, was being surveyed with

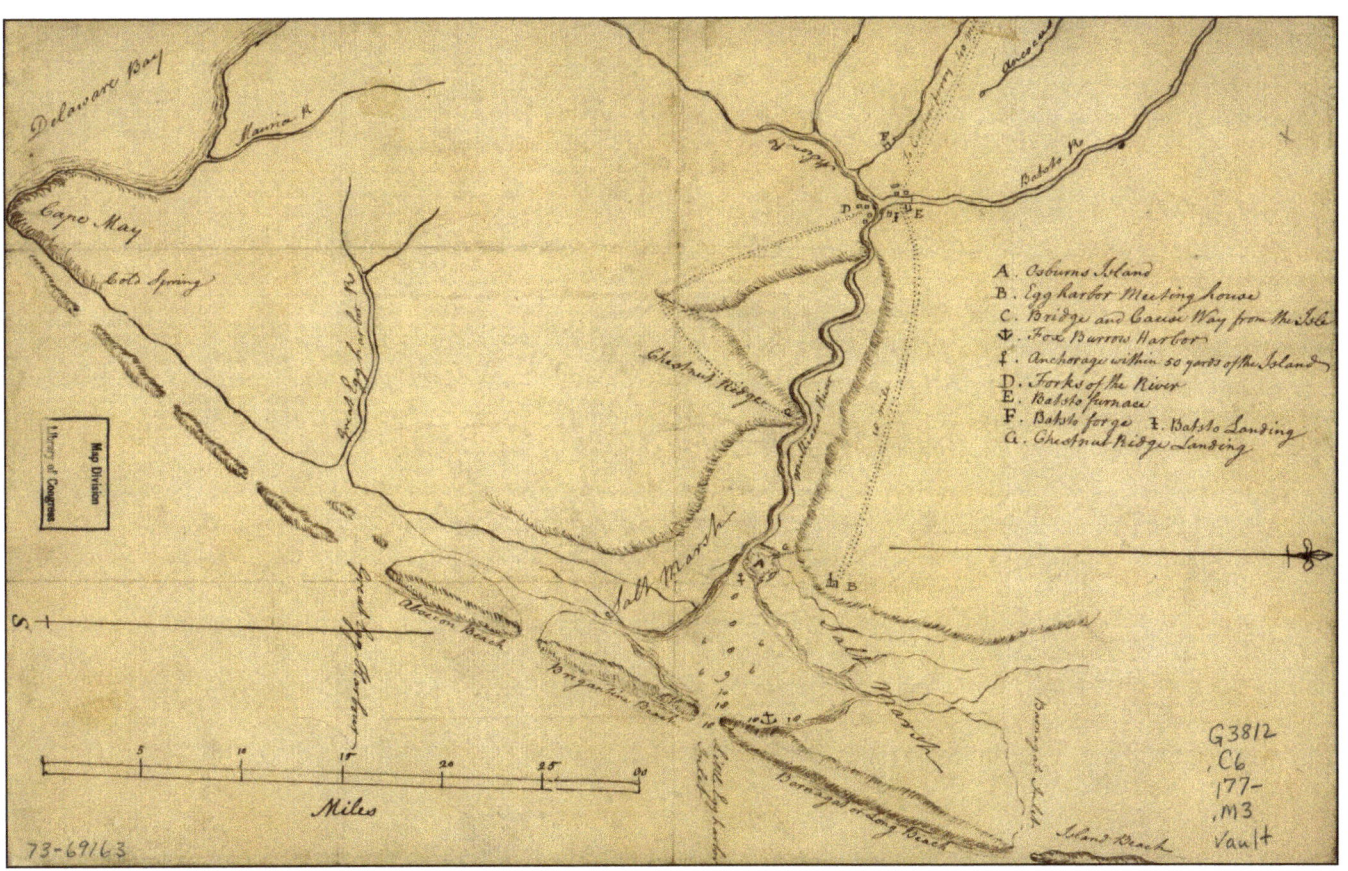

An eighteenth-century map of the Mullica River in New Jersey. *Library of Congress Collection.*

theodolites, parceled into small geometrically uniform lots by land speculators, and opened up by railroads penetrating the deepest reaches of the forests and bogs. These changes are harbingers for the loss of traditional relationships with the land, a base commodification of the intimate knowledge, or *territorialité*, that inhabitants of the Pine Barrens forged over generations with trees, soil, water, and each other.[36] In many ways, this parallels the lament of Henry David Thoreau when he describes the coming of modernity embodied in the disrupting alien whistle of the steam train passing through the woods of Concord in *Walden* (1854).[37] Peterson writes:

> The whole of that section of New Jersey in which the events of our story occurred, has greatly changed since the period of which we write. Sweetwater itself is in decay; the Forks is in ruins; and vast portions of the original forest have fallen before the woodman's axe. A railroad runs close to the place where the hut of the refugee stood; the scream of the locomotive is fast driving away the few deer left in the region. As we send these sheets to press, we notice that a land company is in operation in the neighborhood, and is issuing proposals to furnish "cheap homesteads," according to the approved fashion of these modern associations. All things have changed. If the author has succeeded in describing, however faintly, a region, a society, and a state of manners already nearly eradicated, he will be content to let the genius of improvement complete the work of destruction, and forever remove all traces of the ruder, but more picturesque past.[38]

Like Thoreau, Peterson portrays modernization as an anonymous force acting to eradicate the traditional "sense of place" of the Pine Barrens. Competition from more efficient Pennsylvania (coal-fired) iron furnaces, made more viable through canal and railway transportation, tended, in the long term, to be an important factor in the deindustrialization of the Pine Barrens. The first train steamed its way from Philadelphia to Atlantic City in July 1854, passing just south of Pleasant Mills. Easy access by rail to the heart of the Pine Barrens resulted in rampant land speculation and dreams of new cities, like Egg Harbor City, to be parceled into hundreds of rectangular lots, small farm lots, and peopled by immigrants.

By the late nineteenth century, most of the ironworkers and charcoal producers had left the Pine Barrens. Gone, too, were the horse-drawn stages that took several days to make their way from Philadelphia to the coast, passing inns and taverns built to accommodate the weary and thirsty.[39] New transportation links promised a direct trip between the seashore and the great metropolises of Philadelphia and New York. While modernity brought significant growth to the adjoining coasts of the Pine Barrens, it simultaneously eliminated the need for the many inns and taverns that once dotted the interior of the region.[40] In 1907, New Jersey poet and author Henry van Dyke would record that very conundrum: the coming of the railroad and highway system to the region and the resulting isolation, decline, or abandonment of many Pine Barrens iron villages. In his book *Days Off and Other Digressions*, Van Dyke visits the millpond at Weymouth, a Pine Barrens village some twenty miles southeast of Pleasant Mills:

> After fishing for an hour or two ... we paddled down the pond, which presently widened into quite a lake, ending in a long, low dam with trees

Bog-Iron Furnace/Forge	Founded	Closed
Atsion	1765	ca. 1846
Bamber (Ferrago)	c. 1810	ca. 1865
Batsto	1766	1858
Bergen (ex-Washington)	1832	1854
Birmingham (Retreat)	c. 1800	ca. 1832
Butchers	ca. 1808	1840s
Budd's Iron Works	ca. 1785	ca. 1840
Bordentown	1725	ca. 1750
Cohansie	ca. 1773	pre-1789
Dover	1809	ca. 1868
Ætna (near Tuckahoe)	ca. 1816	1832
Ætna (Medford Lakes)	1766 – 67	1773
Federal Forge	1789	unknown
Federal Furnace	1795	pre-1855
Gloucester	1813	1848
Hampton	pre-1795	ca. 1850
Hanover	1791 – 92	ca. 1864
Lisbon	ca. 1800	ca. 1831
Martha	1793	1840s
Mary Ann	ca. 1827	1860s
Mount Holly	1730	1778
New Mills	1781 – 87	pre-1811
Phoenix	1816 – 17	ca. 1855
Speedwell	ca. 1785	ca. 1839
Taunton	1766 – 67	after 1830
Union	ca. 1800	uncertain
Wading River	1795	1815
Washington (rebuilt as Bergen)	1814	1817
West Creek	1797	1838 – 39
Weymouth	1801 – 02	1862 – 65

Source: Pierce, *Iron in the Pines*, 16-17.

growing all across it. Here was the forgotten village ... once the seat of a flourishing iron industry but now stranded between two railways six miles on either side of it.... [Weymouth] had done nothing to deserve ill fortune. But the timber which had once been floated down its river was all cut and gone; and the bog-iron which had once [been] smelted [in] its furnace was all used up ... and the new colonies of fruit-growers and truck-farmers [from southern Europe] ... did not like to settle quite so far from the railway; and there was nothing for [Weymouth] to do but to sit in the sun and doze, while one family after another melted away, and house after house closed its windows and its doors.[41]

Railroads, theodolites, and developers threatened to change the landscape forever as speculators bought hundreds of thousands of lots in the forests and bogs of the Pine Barrens. However, to the contrary of what Peterson feared in 1855, most of the land remained forested, with ongoing timber harvesting, and thousands of acres converted to cranberry bogs, and still much land remained idle. The infertile sand of the Pine Barrens (excellent for growing pines, cedar, blueberries, and cranberries), coupled with the high-water table that created numerous surface bogs (factors that had first attracted and made the region a continental leader in the production of bog-iron), held little appeal for all but a limited number of charcoal makers, glassblowers, fruit growers, and truck farmers.[42] With the collapse of the bog-iron industry in the 1850s, the land depopulated. With that loss of population, there was an irretrievable loss of collective memory about familiar places.[43] By the turn of the twentieth century, urban hunters from the cities and suburbs of Philadelphia seasonally populated many of the iron villages. In *The Philadelphia Record* of 1915, a journalist visiting Weymouth wrote of how

the wilderness is fast swallowing up what is left of the old village ... [it is] known now to only deer hunters who make the deserted village their headquarters for a few days in the fall and to autoists who catch glimpses of tree-hidden ruins as they speed by on their way to the seashore.[44]

A Resurgent Sense of Place

Despite decreasing population in the decades after the publication of *Kate Aylesford*, the identity and sense of place in the Pine Barrens, far from disappearing under the relentless tug of time and modernity, were being shaped into something completely new by forces that would result in the region's preservation, not as a place of industrial heritage, but as one of America's most dynamic natural and historical regions.[45] In 1876, Philadelphia financier Joseph Wharton, the most important nineteenth-century speculator in Pine Barrens real estate, acquired more than 100,000 acres in the heart of the region, mainly for the rights to the abundant surface water in the area. When the governor of New Jersey made clear that he would impede interstate shipments of water, the Wharton family and its executors held onto the land until the State of New Jersey finally purchased the tract in the 1950s. This "historical and geographical accident," in effect, preserved much of the natural aspects of the forested landscape in a status not so different from what Charles J. Peterson knew in his youth. Today, it is that natural landscape, centered on the villages of Batsto and Pleasant Mills, that has become the core of the Pinelands National Reserve, a landscape now sheltered under preservation laws as a place mainly of natural heritage. A place of industry and commerce in the youth of Peterson, modernity and deindustrialization ironically gave it a new sense of place firmly rooted in the ideal of nature.[46]

From whence does this new ideal originate? In large part, as Peterson unwittingly documented when he wrote of Major Gordon and Kate regularly quitting the city to refresh their connection with nature in the Pine Barrens, and as Henry Charlton Beck and John McPhee much better understood from the vantage point of the twentieth century, it originates from outside the Pines. It is urbanites that see in the Pine Barrens the antithesis of modernity, industrialization, and urbanization. For them, the Pine Barrens provide a connection with nature, and thus a "sense of stability in what is an otherwise continually urbanizing world surrounding the great metropolises of Philadelphia and New York."[47] In this sense, it is hardly surprising that the concepts of "modernity" and "sense of place" should be amongst the principal themes of one of New Jersey's earliest historical romance novels. Over the last 160 years, it is those opposing dualities, which writers such as Peterson, Beck, McPhee, and Bateman all consciously and unconsciously recognized, that have in the long term acted to preserve the Pine Barrens as the antithesis of metropolitan New Jersey—a million-acre "garden in the city" that continues to evoke a powerful sense of "place."

Endnotes

Matthew G. Hatvany is a professor of geography at the Université Laval, North America's second oldest university in Quebec City. He teaches historical geography and regularly accompanies students to the Pine Barrens to compare and contrast this unique natural and cultural region with the surrounding cities of Megalopolis.

1   Charles A. Stansfield Jr., *New Jersey: A Geography* (Boulder: Westview Press, 1983), 204; Charles S. Boyer, *Early Forges and Furnaces in New Jersey* (Philadelphia: University

1. of Pennsylvania Press, 1931); Peter Wacker, "Human Exploitation of the New Jersey Pine Barrens Before 1900," in Richard T. T. Forman, ed., *Pine Barrens: Ecosystem and Landscape* (New Brunswick: Rutgers University Press, 1998), 3-23; Thomas M. Doerflinger, "Rural Capitalism in Iron Country: Staffing a Forest Factory, 1808-1815," *William and Mary Quarterly* 59, 1 (2002): 3-38; Henry Charlton Beck, *Jersey Genesis: The Story of the Mullica River* (New Brunswick: Rutgers University Press, 1945).

2. Arthur D. Pierce, *Iron in the Pines: The Story of New Jersey's Ghost Towns and Bog Iron* (New Brunswick: Rutgers University Press, 1957), 5; J. Albert Starkey Jr., "The Bog Ore and Bog Iron Industry of South Jersey," reprint from "The Bulletin," *New Jersey Academy of Science* 7, 1 (1962): 1; Matthew Hatvany, "Lives of the Bog-Iron Workers: Industry and Community at Martha Furnace," *New Jersey Folklore Society Review* 12 (1991): 3-9.

3. Harriet S. Sander, *Sketches of Old Port Republic* (Port Republic Terecenary Committee, 1964), unpaginated.

4. Charles A. Stansfield Jr., *A Geography of New Jersey: The City in the Garden*, 2nd ed. (New Brunswick: Rutgers University Press, 1998), 1-5; Robert Sullivan, *The Meadowlands: Wilderness Adventures on the Edge of a City* (New York: Doubleday, 1999); John McPhee, "The People of New Jersey's Pine Barrens," *National Geographic* 145, 1 (1974): 52-77.

5. Stansfield, *New Jersey*, 1-8; R. Craig Koedel, *South Jersey Heritage: A Social, Economic and Cultural History* (Lanham, MD: University Press of America, 1979); Richard Velt, "How New Jersey Became a Punchline," *New York Post*, November 4, 2012, http://nypost.com/2012/11/04/how-new-jersey-became-a-punchline/.

6. Charles J. Peterson, *Kate Aylesford: A Story of the Refugees* (Philadelphia: T. B. Peterson and Brothers, 1855), reissued under the pseudonym J. Thornton Randolph, *The Heiress of Sweetwater: A Love Story* (Philadelphia: T. B. Peterson and Brothers, 1873).

    Lydia Maria Child's historical romance "The Youthful Emigrant" (1845) predates *Kate Aylesford* by a decade. A New England writer, Child relies on scant biographical information about Elizabeth Haddon and fictionalizes the account to tell the story of colonization from a female perspective. John Haddon dispatched his seventeen-year-old daughter to the New World when business caused him to remain in England. See L. Maria Child, "The Youthful Emigrant. A True Story of the Early Settlement of New Jersey," *The Columbian Lady's and Gentleman's Magazine* 3, 4 (1845): 241-47.

7. Barrie Hayne, "Standing on Neutral Ground: Charles Jacobs Peterson of 'Peterson's,'" *The Pennsylvania Magazine of History and Biography* 43, 9 (1969): 510.

8. The book was republished in its entirety in 2001 by Plexus Publishing as *Kate Aylesford or The Heiress of Sweetwater*, with a forward by Robert Bateman (Medford, NJ: Plexus Publishing). All references to *Kate Aylesford* are taken from the 2001 edition.

9. Wayne Bodle, "Themes and Directions in Middle Colonies Historiographies, 1980 – 1994," *William and Mary Quarterly* 51, 3 (1994): 355-88.

10. Hayne, "Standing on Neutral Ground."

11. See the biographical sketch of Charles Jacobs Peterson in Karen Nipps, "Charles Jacobs Peterson," *Dictionary of American Biography* 79 (1988): 236-41.

12. David Lowenthal, "Past Time, Present Place: Landscape and Memory," *The Geographical Review* 65, 1 (1975): 1-36; Yi-Fu Tuan, "Place: An Experiential Perspective," *The Geographical Review* 65, 2 (1975): 151-65.

13. H. C. Darby, "The Regional Geography of Thomas Hardy's Wessex," *Geographical Review* 38 (1948): 426-43; L. Anders Sandberg and John S. Marsh, "Focus: Literary Landscapes-Geography and Literature," *The Canadian Geographer* 32, 3 (1988): 266-76; Douglas C. D. Pocock, *Humanistic Geography and Literature* (London: Croom Helm, 1981), 9-19; Claude Raffestin and Mercedes Bresso, "Tradition, Modernité et Territorialité," *Cahiers de Géographie du Québec* 26, 68 (1982): 186-98.

14. *Putnam's Monthly Magazine of American Literature, Science and Art* 6 (July to December, 1855): 104.

15. Robin A. Butlin, *Historical Geography: Through the Gates of Space and Time* (New York: Edward Arnold, 1993), 70.

16. Arthur D. Pierce, *The Elijah Clark Mansion, also Known as The Kate Aylesford Mansion, Home of Mr. and Mrs. Raymond N. Baker, A Sketch of Its History* (The Atlantic County 'Open House Day' of the New Jersey Tercentenary, 1964). It should be noted that in 1971 *The Black Heritage Library Collection* reprinted Peterson's controversial *The Cabin and Parlor; or, Slaves and Masters* (Philadelphia: T. B. Peterson, 1852), written under the pseudonym J. Thornton Randolph.

17. Justin Kaplan, *Walt Whitman: A Life* (Toronto: Bantam Books, 1980), 59.

18. Ann Prestwich, "Charles Jacobs Peterson, Editor and Friend of Lowell and Poe" (Columbia University: MA thesis, 1938), 18; Alfred M. Heston, *South Jersey: A History, 1664 – 1924*, vol. 2 (New York: Lewis Historical Publishing, 1924), 762; Helen Leek Mack, "The Petersons in Philadelphia," genealogical document in the Batsto Library and Archives, Batsto, New Jersey.

19. W. F. Mayer, "In the Pines," *The Atlantic Monthly Magazine* 3 (1859): 560-69; Hatvany, "Lives of the Bog-Iron Workers," 7-8.

20. W. F. Mayer, "In the Pines," *The Atlantic Monthly Magazine* 3 (1859): 560-69; Henry Charlton Beck, *Jersey Genesis: The Story of the Mullica River* (New Brunswick: Rutgers University Press, 1945); John McPhee, *The Pine Barrens* (New York: Ballantine Books, 1967); John McPhee, "The People of New Jersey's Pine Barrens," *National Geographic* 145, 1 (1974): 52-77; Robert Bateman, *Pinelands* (Medford, NJ: Plexus Publishing, 1994).

21. Yi-Fu Tuan, "Place: An Experiential Perspective."

22. The importance of The Forks as a privateer haven and the Battle of Chestnut Neck are detailed in Franklin W. Kemp, *A Nest of Rebel Pirates* (Egg Harbor City, NJ: Batsto Citizens Committee, 1966); see also Barbara Solem-Stull, *The Forks: A Brief History* (Medford, NJ: Plexus Publishing, 2002).

23. Peterson, *Kate Aylesford*, 149.
24. Ibid., 204.
25. Mayer, "In the Pines," 562-3.
26. Vermeule, quoted in Harshberger, *The Vegetation of the New Jersey Pine-Barrens*, 12.
27. Harshberger, *The Vegetation of the New Jersey Pine-Barrens*, 8.
28. Peterson, *Kate Aylesford*, 78.
29. Ibid., 44-45.
30. Beck, *Jersey Genesis*, 287-88.
31. Peterson, *Kate Aylesford*, 45.
32. Ibid., 92.
33. Mack, "The Petersons in Philadelphia." Mack states that "Lawrence Peterson served as a Volunteer in American Army during Revolution. Participated in battle of Trenton and Chestnut Neck," 1. Barbara Solem-Stull also argues that Lawrence Peterson played an important role in shaping Charles Jacobs Peterson's understanding of the Pine Barrens during the Revolutionary War in *The Forks*, 22. Arthur D. Pierce argues in *Iron in the Pines*, 189-90, that the character "Uncle Lawrence" is patterned after Simon Lucas, a Revolutionary veteran who preached at Pleasant Mills "against the vanities of the world." Lucas died in 1838, thus Peterson undoubtedly knew him. Without entering into the debate, it seems probable that Peterson bestowed on Uncle Lawrence the qualities of several different factual persons, as he did for other characters in the book. For more on Lucas, see Charles F. Green, *Pleasant Mills, New Jersey, Lake Nescochague: A Place of Olden Days: An Historical Sketch*, 3rd edition. No place of publication, c. 1929, 17-18.
34. Peterson, *Kate Aylesford*, 188.
35. Ibid., 274.
36. Raffestin and Bresso, "Tradition, Modernité et Territorialité."
37. Henry David Thoreau, *Walden; Or, Life in the Woods* (New York: Dover Publications, 1995), 74-75.
38. Peterson, *Kate Aylesford*, 275-76.
39. Charles S. Boyer, *Old Inns and Taverns in West Jersey* (Camden, NJ: Camden County Historical Society, 1962).
40. Stansfield, *A Geography of New Jersey*, 164-65.
41. Henry van Dyke, quoted in Robert F. Johnson, *Weymouth New Jersey: A History of the Furnace, Forge, and Paper Mills* (Kearney, NE: Morris Publishing, 2001), 86-87.
42. Wacker, "Human Exploitation of the New Jersey Pine Barrens"; Kenryu Hashikawa, "Rural Enterprise and the Northern Economy in the Early Republic: The New Jersey Charcoal Venture as a Test Case," *The Japanese Journal of American Studies* 15 (2004): 97-113; Mark Demitroff, "Sugar Sand Opportunity: Landscape and People of the Pine Barrens," *Vernacular Architecture Newsletter* (Summer 2014).
43. Rita Zorn Moonsammy, David Steven Cohen and Lorrain E. Williams, eds., *Pinelands Folklife* (New Brunswick: Rutgers University Press, 1987), 60-61.
44. Quoted in Johnson, *Weymouth*, 93-94.
45. Forman, *Pine Barrens*.
46. On the ideal of nature see Roderick Nash, *Wilderness and the American Mind*, 4th ed. (New Haven: Yale University Press, 2001).
47. Moonsammy et al., *Pinelands Folklife*, 60-61.

Othello, New Jersey. A group of men gather outside of David J. Statham's store in the small settlement of Othello, Greenwich Township, Cumberland County, on a mid-winter's late morning. The building that once housed the store still stands at the northeast corner of Sheppards Mill Road and Ye Greate Street and is a private residence today. Also known as Head of Greenwich, Othello nucleated around a tavern once occupying the Ewing-Bacon House, located at 329 Old Mill Road in the village. Othello is situated northwest of Greenwich and due west of Springtown, a refuge community for fugitive slaves in the antebellum days.

The Newest SJCHC Titles

The South Jersey Culture & History Center proudly announces the release of *Burlington Biographies: A History of Burlington, New Jersey told through the Lives and Times of its People* by Robert L. Thompson. The study takes a fresh look at many aspects of the city's rich heritage and longstanding lore, sometimes strengthening well-known historical accounts, but also toppling a number of commonly held myths extending back a century or more. This 558-page hardbound book will delight, entertain, and intrigue both the reader who possesses knowledge of Burlington and its story and the neophyte who seeks to learn more about a community that intrepid Quaker founders settled in the second half of the seventeenth century. Topics include African American history, the American War for Independence, architecture, artisanal work, city planning, immigration, merchants, and prior local historians, among many others.

Bob Thompson began writing this history about twenty-five years ago while an employee of the city. He contributed articles to the *Burlington Story*, a local history pamphlet published by Dr. Bisbee, Mr. Thompson's mentor. These articles, updated and augmented, form the basis for much of this study.

The title can be purchased for $30.00 from Second Time Books, 114 Creek Road, Mount Laurel, NJ 08054 (856) 234-9335 or ordered directly from the South Jersey Culture & History Center.

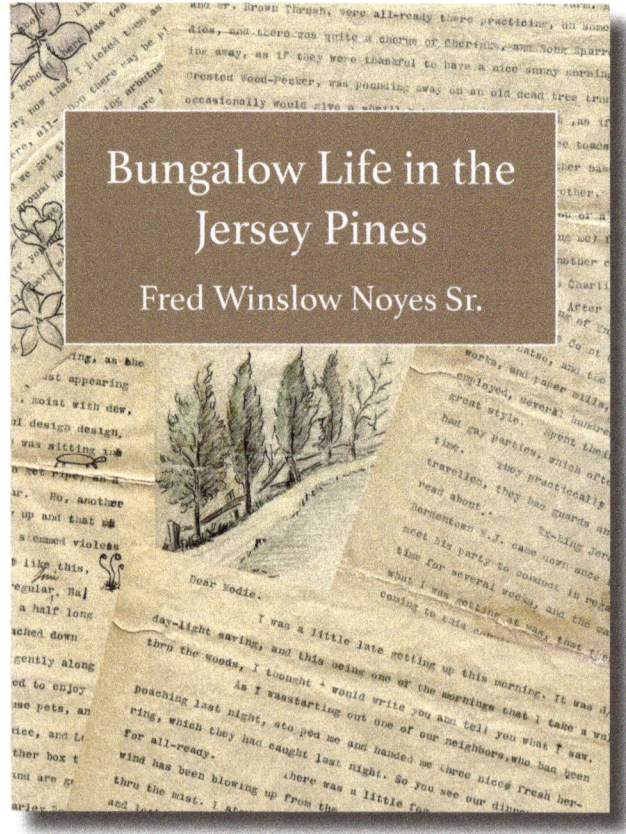

Bungalow Life in the Jersey Pines is a collection of letters written during the spring of 1933 by Fred Winslow Noyes Sr. to his niece. These colorful letters quite literally illustrate life in the Jersey Pines along the Mullica River. They provide a window into the life of Fred Noyes Sr., mayor of Lower Bank, New Jersey, and father of Fred Noyes Jr., who along with his wife Ethel, founded the Towne of Historic Smithville, New Jersey, and the Noyes Museum of Stockton University. With an introduction by Kyle Ewers and afterword by Judy Courter.

This 24-page pamphlet is available directly from the South Jersey Culture & History Center for $5.00.

Alfred and Muriel:
The Story of the J. A. Sweeton House in Cherry Hill, New Jersey

Brian Stolz as told by Jim Stanton

John Alfred Sweeton as a Commander, USN. *Courtesy of Nancy Pille.*

Muriel Sweeton enjoying an open field. *Courtesy of Nancy Pille.*

Frank Lloyd Wright (1867 – 1959), the prominent twentieth-century American architect, is a household name to anyone with an interest in home design. Wright's architectural work includes 25 National Historic Landmarks scattered across the United States. The American Institute of Architects has recognized him as the greatest American architect of all time. While commended for his international projects (such as the Second Imperial Hotel in Tokyo), Wright gained greater renown for his contributions to domicile architecture. He developed his own aesthetic known as the Usonian style, named for its roots in United States urban planning, which prioritizes both the utility and affordability of a residence. Wright believed in the *Nature* of his work, capitalizing the word to emphasize its value as an essence of reality. To Wright, Nature referred to the correlation between architecture and the elements of a building's natural surroundings: he aimed to embody the settings of his homes within their design. The Fallingwater residence, located southeast of Pittsburgh, is one of his best-known designs and—with its cascading, stone-like façade that mirrors the underflowing waterfall—exemplifies how the architect utilized the surrounding environment to draw inspiration for his plans. Fallingwater's design and construction costs ran very high, however, and for that reason was not rendered in Wright's Usonian style. Many of Wright's lesser-known projects better illustrate his philosophy of design, and are themselves testaments to the Nature in which Wright believed.

The J. A. Sweeton House in Cherry Hill is one of four Wright-designed houses constructed in the Garden State. It is the smallest and (as it stands) a passerby might not realize its significance to architectural history. It is an enigma. What could have tempted a world-class architect to build upon this unimposing, seven-acre tract of land? What caused Wright to scale down his designs from their usual dimensions? Jim Stanton, engineer and resident of Sweetwater, New Jersey, is one of the few who can illuminate the story of this curious house. Along with his wife Linda, Stanton has personal ties to the history of South Jersey; the couple organizes and runs *Lines on the Pines*, an annual event that brings together artists, authors, and advocates of the Pinelands. As for the Sweeton House, Stanton is the nephew of its commissioner and namesake—"Uncle Alfred," Stanton calls him. "*John* Alfred Sweeton, but nobody knew that until they saw his mail!"

Serving as an electrical engineer in the United States Navy for over thirty years, Sweeton rose to the rank of captain. At the age of sixteen, he entered Annapolis, having left high school early and completed his secondary education on his own. Self-motivated, Sweeton finished Annapolis near the top of his class and received a Master's Degree from the Massachusetts Institute of Technology in Naval Architecture and Marine Engineering. Thirty years of military service did not wear down the resilient engineer, and he continued his work on naval vessels long after his retirement from the Navy. Stanton witnessed his uncle's resolve firsthand: "I can remember when Uncle Alfred was around the seventy-year old range, and they had a house in Ship Bottom . . . he would go out to the ocean to go swimming before the lifeguards came on—because they didn't let you out far enough!"

Stanton also remembers that his Aunt Muriel, Sweeton's wife, was as much a contrast to her husband as a compliment. While Alfred adhered to the habits of a military man, she was inclined to promote the arts. Stanton recalls her involvement in the Long Beach Island Foundation for the Arts and Sciences (though he is unsure where the sciences fit in). She was kindhearted and intelligent, but the complete opposite from an engineer—a different cut of cloth than Alfred or their nephew. Yet being as opposed as Yin and Yang, the two Sweetons were just as compatible.

Nancy Pille, the Sweetons' daughter, describes her parents' unique blend of creativity and coordination. She remembers that when her father became involved with the 1939 salvage of the submarine SQUALUS, husband and wife tested pontoon logistics using a water-filled roasting pan on a coffee table. Their contrasting personalities aided the couple in achieving their goals, but the driving force behind the completion of the Sweeton House was not the straight-backed captain or the two together. It was Muriel.

Long before the couple laid plans for the house, Muriel became fascinated with Wright's Usonian style. Before her marriage to Alfred, she brought him to a Wright presentation in New York City circa 1930. The couple then travelled across the world for Alfred's duty assignments—China, Burma, the Philippines—the Sweeton family was even escorted back to the United States in a Navy convoy when World War II began. But the tenacious Muriel never lost her love for the architect's style. According to Stanton, "She had been all over the world with my uncle in the Navy . . . and she had decided somewhere along the line that she really wanted a house designed by Frank Lloyd Wright." As a testament to her determination, Alfred Sweeton finished his military service between the years 1948 and 1949. Construction of the house began in 1950.

Of course, Frank Lloyd Wright was not the type of professional who would answer just anyone's summons. It took roughly three years of correspondence for the architect to concede, and gaining his cooperation proved

The J. A. Sweeton House is notably horizontally oriented, as apparent by its roofing and ranch-like design. *Courtesy of Dan Nichols, AIA.*

Alfred and Muriel

A contemporary picture of the J. A. Sweeton House with its prominent carport overhang to the right. *Courtesy of Dan Nichols, AIA.*

no easy task for the Sweetons. When Wright initially proved noncompliant, Muriel changed her tack and found a beneficial ally in Olga, Wright's wife. Muriel and Olga had met at a conference of handweavers, and while Stanton is not certain about the exact nature of the relationship between the two—"I don't know if pester is the right word"—he is certain that the former's daring paid off: "Apparently every so often Wright's wife would say, 'honey, what about the Sweeton House?' And ultimately persistence resulted in getting him to design a house for them." Imposing odds had been overcome and Wright, now lovingly referred to by the Sweetons as "the old man" (he was 83 at the time), acquiesced to design and build their home in Cherry Hill.

The Sweetons purchased a seven-acre plot of land for the home in the midst of a peach orchard. Samuel DeCou, the seller, was one of many farmers in the region. The DeCou, DeCosta, Collins, and Lafferty families—Alfred and Muriel's neighbors-to-be—owned about 2,000 acres apiece. It was amidst this agrarian community that Wright built his new project. The Sweetons struck a deal with farmer DeCou: peach harvests would continue on Sweeton property for a set number of years, but no new trees would be planted. For the Sweetons, the deal was sweetened by unlimited access to fresh peaches. Stanton remembers "going out with wooden bushel baskets, filling as many up as we could, and taking them home . . . they were better than anything you could ever get." Aside from peaches, the property also offered a bounty of forsythia that the Sweetons would gather and force by filling a bathtub with steamy water. Nancy recalls her disgruntled father, heading to the shower, only to find a tub filled with forsythia. One could not think of a more welcoming place to establish a new home.

Typically, when Wright designed a project, one of his interns or associates would remain on-site to oversee its completion. Given the unique relation between Wright and the Sweetons, however, it is no surprise that their situation differed from the norm. Though Stanton argues Uncle Alfred never let on much about his funds or spending, the couple's financial preferences seem to have affected Wright's design process. To circumvent the standard cost of room, board, and travel for one of the architect's apprentices, the Sweetons kept in touch with Wright and his assistant Allen L. ("Davy") Davison through mail and the occasional phone call. Davy had been assigned to shepherd the project to completion after Wright's initial design.

Stanton is also convinced that the Sweetons had a hand in the atypical blueprint. Given Alfred's engineering skills and Muriel's artistic talents, it does seem likely that the couple had a measurable influence on the home's design. Nancy relates that her father worked side by side with Davy, and Muriel was responsible for weaving the fabric of the original drapes and furniture.

The Sweeton House is unusual in its deviation from Wright's typical dimensions of design. Easily the smallest of the four Wright homes built in New Jersey, it is possible that the residence's size was restricted by an agreed upon cost: the standard minimum price for a Wright house at the time was roughly $30,000, but the final cost of the Sweeton House fell considerably below that figure. Furthermore, original designs for the home placed it at the edge of an embankment on the property, but the soil failed a slump test, meaning it would not sustain the structure's weight, and Wright revised the plans to stabilize the house on flat land. Consisting of a living room, three bedrooms, and one bath, all organized in a horizontally-oriented layout, the Sweeton House might incline one to overlook its structure: "Back then, you wouldn't call it a modern design. The outside, the roof, was relatively flat with straight lines: nothing sticking out," Stanton observes, "It's a one-story, ranch-like design. Concrete floors—I think they were red—the heat was in the floor, radiant heat." Starting with the floors, Stanton identifies one of the many features that make the residence part of Wright's legacy and begins to unravel just what makes it novel.

With deference to its architect's fondness for Nature, the red concrete floors (Chinese red) in the Sweeton House—complimented by the use of redwood plywood—may very well reflect the sheen of peaches in the surrounding orchard; Wright held radiators and ductwork in disdain, so the unified heating in the floor was not uncommon for his designs. The high walls, floor-to-ceiling windows, and mitered glass corners of the house leave it very open to its surroundings, also a typical facet of Wright's style. Many elements of the house (such as its mobile chairs) are built into the walls, and the furniture (such as a three-piece redwood table) is as much a part of the architectural planning as the infrastructure.

These unique stylings are likely due to the architect's philosophy of form following function, but if that were the case, Stanton might have a question or two for Wright about the Nature of the fireplace: "It was a fireplace that had a back wall and a side wall and it was open on two sides . . . so how do you get the smoke to go up that sucker?" Wright's disregard of the norm is pardonable, given his talent, and, of course, the fireplace works without a hitch. Stanton's curiosity about several other aspects of the Sweeton House is nevertheless well-grounded. Most anyone would raise an eyebrow at one particularly harrowing choice Wright made regarding the carport.

Looming ominously over whatever unfortunate object rests beneath it, the carport is not only one of the most interesting aspects of the Sweeton House, but presumably a miracle of science. To use the technical term, it is cantilevered, but that descriptor fails to indicate just how precarious the jutting cover feels. In fact, the construction of the carport stood as one of the most daunting obstacles to many contractors, most of whom passed on the project because of it. Stanton recalls the confusion it instilled: "Our next-door neighbor was a custom builder . . . he looked at it and said, 'I don't know how they're gonna make that stay up there. I'm pretty sure I can't do that.'" After besting the nerves of several contractors, the carport was eventually unable to scare off a builder by the name of Draper from Haddonfield and he finished the project just as Wright envisioned it. Two steel beams running through the structure were anchored to the foundation with steel rods. One cannot ignore that when the Sweetons sold the house in the early 1970s no sag had occurred in the carport. There is none to this day.

It is hard to deny that, whether it was Wright's intention or not, both Alfred and Muriel are in some way memorialized in the Sweeton House. Down to earth and emphatically horizontal in orientation, the structure is just as likely a comment on South Jersey topography as it is on the veteran's direct and squared away persona. Similarly, the home's flashier elements (including a personalized space for craftwork) stand as tribute to the artistic and creative Muriel. The miracle carport resembles both Alfred's poise and his wife's determination, and much as the couple was a force to be reckoned with, so too is the home they helped build—one of the few legacies America's best architect left in New Jersey. Their Nature (as Wright viewed it) certainly lives on within the Sweeton Residence.

As time passes, it may be that the J. A. Sweeton House will only be remembered as another Frank Lloyd Wright project; however, the quirky residence owes its existence to Alfred and Muriel Sweeton as much as it does to the famous architect. Stanton attended his Aunt Muriel's memorial service, and remembers how "the guy who owned the house at the time was an architect . . . and he did a little talk about it; part of it was Aunt Muriel, and how she got this house built, because if it wasn't for her he wouldn't be able to live there in a Frank Lloyd Wright house." The gratitude displayed here for Muriel (and, by extension, Alfred) is testament to how their character is imbued in the home: one cannot understand the full story of the Sweeton House without knowing the character of the Sweetons.

When Stanton attended a birthday celebration for local historian Paul W. Schopp in 2013, he offhandedly mentioned their vicinity to his uncle's old house—built by the famous Frank Lloyd Wright. Schopp's attention sparked, and he immediately responded, "The Sweeton House?!" One might argue Alfred and Muriel's spirit shone through on the spot; so long as their namesake sits on that tract of land in Cherry Hill, their mark on the area will never truly fade away.

NOTE

During a pleasant afternoon meeting along the banks of the Mullica River, at the Sweetwater Marina and Riverdeck, Jim Stanton related the story of Alfred and Muriel's Frank Lloyd Wright house to Tom Kinsella, who was enthralled by the account and asked for permission to assign a Stockton editing intern to research and fill in details. The task fell to Brian T. Stolz, who in December 2016 graduated from Stockton University with Cum Laude honors. Special thanks go to Nancy Pille and Dan Nichols who explained details about the Sweetons, the Sweeton house, and provided images.

SoJourn

THE SOUTH JERSEY COLLECTIONS AT STOCKTON

Within the last year, the Special Collections & Archives department of the Bjork Library at Stockton University has acquired three manuscript collections of significant local interest.

The **Rebecca Estell Bourgeois collection** features hundreds of letters, deeds, and documents pertaining to southern Atlantic County, especially the area around Estell Manor. Dating from the mid-eighteenth century through the first third of the twentieth century, this material documents the Estell glassworks, local boat-building and shipping industries, and several generations of the Estell family's property acquisitions.

(below) the Estell Glassworks.

The **Bjork Library Special Collections & Archives** are open Monday through Friday, 8:00am – 4:00pm. For an appointment to review these and other South Jersey collections at Stockton University, please contact Louise Tillstrom at (609) 652-4532 or via email at Louise.Tillstrom@stockton.edu.

The majority of the **Evans and Wills collection** comprises the business records of berry growers Evans and Wills from incorporation in 1930 through the company's dissolution in the mid 1960s. In addition, there are many older invoices such as those seen above.

The **Wading River collection** includes day books kept by the McKeens and others pertaining to river freighting and cartage (see page to the right) and also holds records of Samuel S. Downs who surveyed land throughout the Little Egg Harbor area during the nineteenth century.

School Segregation in the Post-Civil War Era:
Burlington County, New Jersey, 1865 – 1915

Zachary T. Baer

Upon a verdant unused schoolyard situated nearly a mile from Burlington City's portion of the Delaware River, sits an extant reminder of New Jersey's racially discriminant past. Known as the William R. Allen School, the brick structure was erected in 1900 to replace the Federal Street School, where the city's black children had been educated since 1870. Expanded in 1914 and again in 1924, the Allen School served as a bastion of segregated education for scores of black teachers and black students working and living in Burlington. At the school, and within the district, segregation remained present until 1948, when district superintendent Dr. Joseph W. Howe and school board president Mrs. Frank K. Brotherton elicited help from a *de facto* group of leaders, including the National Association for the Advancement of Colored People (NAACP), a recently established local Citizens Committee, and the Burlington City School Board to integrate the district's schools.[1]

Burlington's relatively smooth school integration process may come as a surprise to readers, considering the city racially comingled its school population not out of threat, but based on its own sovereignty. The united effort of Howe, Brotherton, the NAACP, the Citizens Committee, and the City School Board, however, succeeded at something previously attempted nearly 65 years earlier by Jeremiah H. Pierce, minister of the local Bethlehem African Methodist Episcopal church (AME). During the 1880s, Pierce won a court battle in the New Jersey Supreme Court titled *The State, Ex Rel. Jeremiah H. Pierce vs. The Union District Trustees*, which allowed Pierce to send his children to the all-white schools in Burlington City. This article will follow Pierce's fight against school segregation by contextualizing the court case within the larger educational framework present at that time. In doing so, it will illustrate that Pierce's approach to education was antithetical to his era's approach to the topic, led by individuals such as Booker T. Washington, which tolerated segregation and encouraged vocational education. As a result of Washington's dominant educational pedagogy, Pierce's case failed to aid black youth beyond just his own children.

Pierce pre-dates the two federal Supreme Court cases that dominate the traditional narrative surrounding American school segregation: *Plessy v. Ferguson* (1896), which cemented the "separate-but-equal" doctrine, and *Brown v. Board of Education of Topeka* (1954), which declared "separate-but-equal" a violation of the Fourteenth Amendment's Equal Protection Clause. Of the two cases, *Brown* is the most pertinent because it served as a catalyst for desegregation efforts in countless school districts nationwide, which advances an important question: why did *Brown* become a landmark decision while *Pierce* did not? Robert Korstad and Nelson Lichtenstein examine *Brown's* success in "Opportunities Found and Lost," linking its impact on public schools nationwide to two factors: a widespread, organized national citizenry movement and support from the federal government. In their words, *Brown* was "a dead letter until given political force by a growing protest movement."[2] Thus, they conclude that a movement without proper organizational backing will fail to impact society—an important rule to consider while examining *Pierce*.

Over the decades following the *Pierce* decision, several monographs and articles detailing the case have entered the scholarly marketplace. This scholarship largely argues that *Pierce* failed to accomplish school-wide desegregation.[3] For example, Ernest Lyght writes in *Path to Freedom* that following *Pierce*, "... almost all of the Negro school children attended the Allen School."[4] Interestingly, though the prevailing attitude shaped by writers like Lyght largely downplays *Pierce*, it is commonplace for modern narratives to praise the case's outcome. An article published in the *Asbury Park Press* in 1982 declares *Pierce*, "a landmark decision that was crucial to the struggle for civil rights in New Jersey"; while a more scholarly tome asserts, "The court's decision in Pierce's favor marked one of the most important civil rights gains in the state's history...."[5]

The result of each analytical work, scholarly and non-scholarly alike, leaves the reader viewing *Pierce's* legacy as simultaneously a failure and a landmark decision. In such an obfuscated state, Pierce's case bids a fresh examination. While some scholars designate *Pierce* as a "landmark case" due to the New Jersey Supreme Court's issuing a *writ of mandamus*, the case had no visible impact on public school segregation and was merely a personal victory for Pierce and his children. Twelve years later, *Plessy v. Ferguson* vacated any hope of *Pierce* initiating widespread change. The lack of success from *Pierce* does not fall upon the claimant's shoulders. Instead, it reflects the era's disparate educational philosophies and the paucity of legal, institutional and organizational support during the post-civil war era. Pierce's valiant fight simply occurred at the wrong time, preceding the formation of empowerment groups like the NAACP, which played a pivotal role in twentieth-century desegregation efforts.

BLACK EDUCATION IN BURLINGTON COUNTY BEFORE *PIERCE*

Black education in Burlington County preceding *Pierce* was marked by an increase in educational opportunities for children of color, led in large part by New Jersey state legislators. Beginning in 1844, the legislators passed a new state constitution establishing a statewide school system, including an appropriation for a School Fund to support public schools "for the equal benefit of all the people of the state."[6] The following year, the state utilized the School Fund to appoint a state superintendent devoted to "elevating the condition of schools and informing the public."[7] As state superintendent T. F. King recognized in 1847, elevating the schools was no easy task. It meant juggling a plethora of issues plaguing the school system, including inadequate teachers, a need for school examiners, greater cohesion between state and local districts, and most importantly—additional schools.[8] In several municipalities in Burlington County, students relied upon tuition-based schools or sectarian facilities. Local Sunday schools, private academies, and formal schools served as the bulwark for the education system, e.g., Baptists established the Burlington Institution in 1834, comprising a campus of over six acres. However, the school remained in operation for only seven years.[9]

In this environment, a student's school experience depended upon his or her place of residence and/or skin color. A student living in an urban district, compared to a rural district, attended school more frequently. For example, Burlington City's schools remained open for ten months in 1850, while Southampton, a rural township in Burlington County, opened for just over seven months. Furthermore, laws did not require students to attend school, so attendance varied from urban to rural districts. In 1850, 62% of Burlington City's school-aged children received at least some level of education during the school year, compared to 41.4% in neighboring rural Chester Township, where schooling came second to agriculture.[10]

Underlying the intricate influence of legislators, local leaders, and laws on local schools was the presence of racism. During the nascent years of the formal school movement, religious groups like the Quakers often designated schools for black children. However, not all black children received a segregated education. In certain rural communities, black children learned alongside white children. Dr. James Still, an autodidactic black doctor from rural Burlington County, provides an account of his experience in an integrated school in South Jersey during the 1830s:

> I was about eight or nine years old when I first was sent to school, and this was a new era to me. I soon became acquainted with all of the children, but their sports were not pleasure to me. At most of the plays I was a poor hand. I learned none of them, not even so much as a game of marbles, and at ball I was only chosen to make up the number.
>
> We went to school only in bad weather, and worked during the fair weather. There was one thing I soon learned, and that was to curse and to swear, although this was never known to my parents. Our school-books were the New Testament and Comly's Spelling-Book, in which we learned everything that was useful for man

Table 1

Burlington County, New Jersey – 1860				
Municipality	Population	Number of Black Students	Total Number of Students (age 5 – 18)	School
Burlington City	5,174	40	997	Segregated
Bordentown Borough	4,027	69	932	Segregated
Evesham	3,145	66	968	Segregated
Northampton	2,997	29	550	-
Mansfield	2,777	18	unknown	-
Cinnaminson/Chester[11]	2,701/2,227	40	1416	Segregated
Pemberton	2,672	10	600	-

Sources: *Annual Report of the Superintendents of Public Schools* (1860), 66. Superintendent of the Census Department, Abstract of Population and Statistics of the State of New Jersey, According to the Census of 1860 (Trenton, NJ: Phillips and Boswell Printers, 1862), 4. Louis Kaser, *A Story of the Public Schools of Burlington County* (Riverton, NJ: Press of the New Era, 1943).

to know. The teacher taught us grammar in those books, and taught us how to pronounce everything improperly, and we knew no better. I am glad that in these days a better order of things is instituted in our own State, and that the merit of a teacher is known before being employed.[12]

As New Jersey's total population increased and free black families settled throughout the state, the racial divide grew more apparent. Table 1 provides a data matrix displaying the seven most populated constituencies in Burlington County in descending order, derived from the 1860 United States Census and the 1860 State Superintendent's Report. The table shows a relationship between total population, black students, and segregation. The data indicates that districts with both a significant total pupil population and a large number of black students tended to have segregated schools, while less populated rural districts contained integrated schools. The data also suggests that districts in Burlington County with at least 40 black students typically established a segregated school. Finally, the table suggests segregated schools occurred primarily in urban centers; however, further geographical and demographic research is required to verify this argument.[13]

In the coming decades, state legislators continued to enact a concatenation of reform that would intertwine the expansion of public schools with increased educational opportunities for black children:

1) In 1867, state legislators approved a general tax to support public schools.
2) In 1871, New Jersey Governor Theodore Fitz Randolph worked with state legislators to secure free schools funded through public taxes and under the state's aegis.[14]
3) In 1874, state legislators passed a school law requiring children ages eight through thirteen to attend school for at least twelve weeks out of the school year.[15] This series of laws—bringing free public schools and demanding mandatory attendance—caused school attendance to skyrocket. Between 1870 and 1880, school attendance in Burlington County increased by 1,497, or 16.4%.[16] In Camden County, Burlington County's neighbor, attendance increased by 4,398, or 53.7%.[17] This surge in school attendance helped establish New Jersey's system of school segregation.

While the exact provenance of the first black school in Burlington City is unknown, the historic record indicates that by 1866 black students living in the district would have attended a segregated school on Wood Street. Because Burlington City remained predominantly Caucasian, white students attended separate, well-maintained schools throughout the city.[18] The unequal and segregated facilities that school officials established served as a source of tension for many of the city's black residents. Capturing this acrimony, Reverend Theodore Gould, pastor of the city's Bethlehem African Methodist Episcopal Church (AME), wrote a squib in an 1866 edition of *The Dollar Newspaper*, published in Burlington. He asked, "When the well constructed and commodious brick building was erected on Stacy street below Union, was the appropriation made with the express understanding that this house was for the white children, or was it for all? Were not all taxed to pay for this building?"[19]

Evidently, Gould's complaints encouraged Burlington officials to organize the construction of a new school for black children. By 1867, a trio of city officials acquired and subsequently conveyed land for the Trustees of the Union District of Burlington City, leading to the erection of the Federal Street School for black students in 1870.[20] With the construction of a new, segregated school, officials ensured their segregationist policies endured.

Against Systematic Segregation: Jeremiah H. Pierce in Burlington

In late February 1881, the teacher at the "colored school" in Fair Haven, Monmouth County, New Jersey, resigned. The school trustees then closed the school and transferred all of the African American children to the white school.[21] These events caused hard feelings on both sides of the color line.[22] "The whites opposed this mingling of the races, but voted that a new school be built for colored children.... The colored people are indignant and will insist that their children be admitted to the white school."[23] In response to this issue, Republican State Senator James Youngblood introduced a supplement to the 1874 School Act, stating, "no child, between the age of five and eighteen years of age, shall be excluded from any public school in this state on account of his or her religion, nationality, or color.[24] The bill passed the legislative process on March 17, 1881.[25] Although this was a significant step forward, the new law proved ineffective, as most superintendents simply ignored it.[26] The dialectical opposition between black and white communities—manifested by the events at Fair Haven—highlighted a destructive milieu of systematic segregation prevalent within many South Jersey communities.

Jeremiah Pierce was no stranger to such racial animus. As a black minister in the AME New Jersey Annual Conference, he experienced this contention during his ministerial career throughout New Jersey. Pierce was born in Bridgeton Township, Cumberland County, New Jersey, in 1841 to Adrian and Rachel Pierce. Jeremiah's family lived on a farm in Gouldtown—a small-unincorporated free black settlement approximately a mile east of Bridgeton.[27] Gouldtown reportedly traces its origin to the granddaughter of Quaker leader and founder of Salem, John Fenwick. Her name was Elizabeth Adams, and reportedly she scandalously settled in the area now comprising Gouldtown with one of her Grandfather's black slaves named Gould.[28] Like many Gouldtown residents, the 1850 census enumerator designated Pierce a "mulatto," and a member of a large family composed of siblings Stewart, Emma, Isabella, and Elizabeth.[29] Because Gouldtown was a free black community during the pre-emancipation period, most residents spent their whole lives in the town. Profitable farms—devised from generation to generation—dotted the landscape, creating a tightly knit community comprised of two predominant surnames: Gould and Pierce.[30] Like most Gouldtown inhabitants, Pierce worked his father's farm as a young adult. Census records indicate he received some level of educational training in adolescence. A subscription for $1 in 1862 to the main organ of the AME church, *The Christian Recorder*, indicates his concern for the publication's slogan: "religion, morality, literature, and science."[31] Three years later, on December 25, 1865, Pierce married Hannah H. Gould and for the next ten years worked on his own farm in Gouldtown.[32]

Because Gouldtown remained exclusively a black settlement, Pierce lived a relatively sheltered life until venturing from Gouldtown to the Philadelphia Annual Conference to be ordained into the AME church in 1875. A short time after, the Bishop of the Philadelphia Conference transferred him to the newly organized New Jersey Annual Conference, where he would remain a minister for the rest of his life.[33] Pierce pastored in different regions of New Jersey, including a stint in Woodstown, Salem County, New Jersey, where he went toe-to-toe with school trustees in a successful bout to send his children to the town's all-white school.[34] After three years, the Annual Conference appointed Pierce to the Bethlehem AME church in Burlington City. On May 10, 1883, Pierce and his family moved into their home at 136 East Pearl Street.[35] According to the historic record, once settled, a local school trustee arrived at Pierce's house to enroll his children into the school system. Noticing the color of their skin, the trustee instinctively wrote a single permit for all four children to attend the "colored" Federal Street School located near Earle Street, which he justified by stating it was against the rules to permit colored children into white schools, so he "was not disposed to break the rule."[36] With immediate ire, Pierce purportedly responded:

"I suppose if my children were white you would give me permits and at once?"

"O, yes," was the reply; "but as it is I cannot. I admit that it is your right if you choose to contend for it, but I think you will have some trouble before you succeed."

I then called on another. He expressed his willingness, but realized that he would be alone

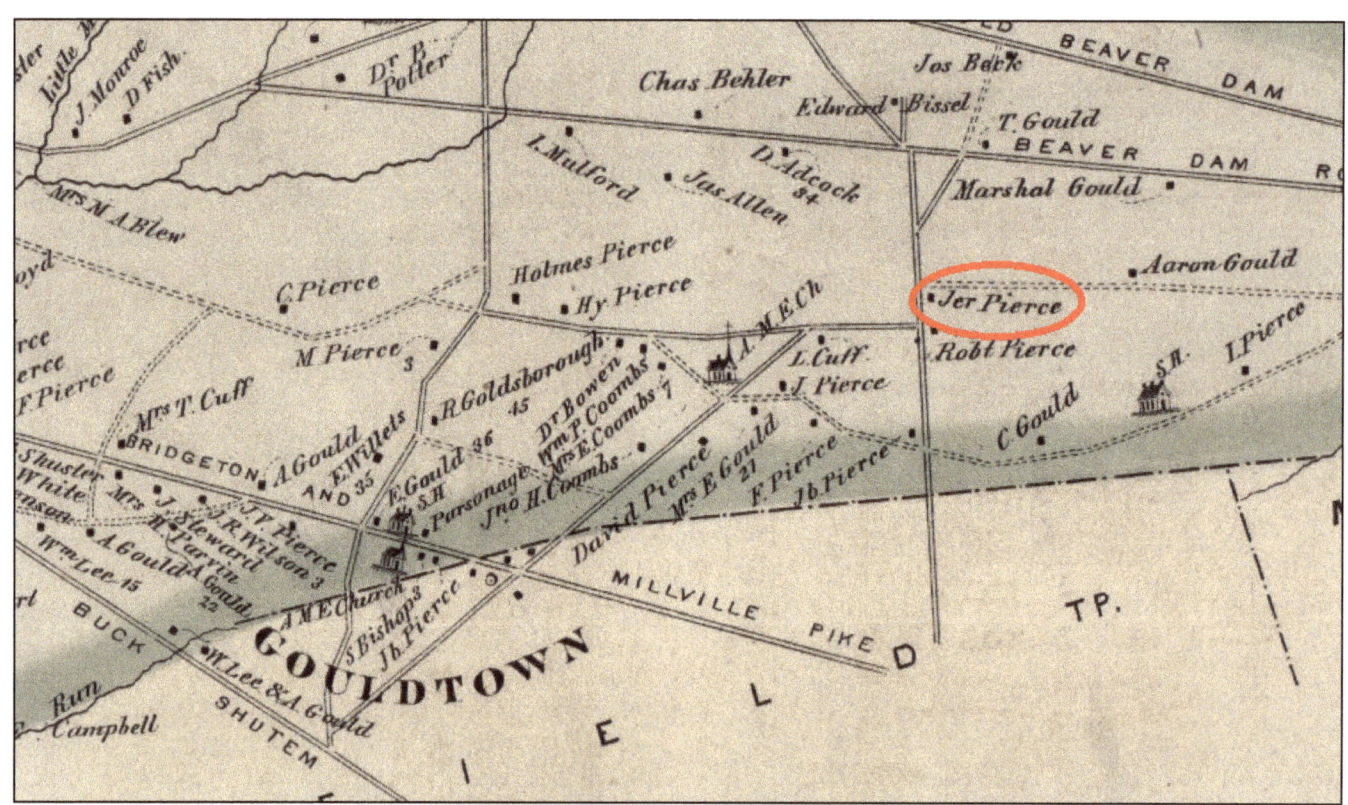

Detail of Bridgeton Township from D. L. Stewart's *Combination Atlas Map of Cumberland County, New Jersey*, 1876.

in the effort. I then called on the third, and he could not seem to realize that I belonged to the human race, and positively declared that no colored child would ever get into the white schools in Burlington by his vote, and, further, that he would be very sorry to see the day when colored children can go to school with the white in this city, "for," said he "I have a little boy of my own that I shall want to send to school some of these days, and should be very sorry to have him go with colored children. I am a good Republican, too," was his remark....[37]

As if blatant racism was not enough, the Federal Street School offered Pierce's children much more limited educational opportunities. An 1883 report states that a single teacher managed fifty students and taught nine different subjects.[38] In addition, Pierce described the school's physical attributes as "one small class room on the first floor that is of any service, while the second story is unfinished and can only be reached by the use of an old ladder, and that quite tottering...."[39] With the school in such a derisory state, few black students received their high school diploma in Burlington, further reinforcing the false notion that black students could not "acquire literary knowledge like white children."[40]

Finding the educational standards wholly inadequate, Pierce sent his four children to both the Stacy and St. Mary Street School in June 1883, where the Principal refused to admit each child due to the color of their skin.[41] Upon their refusal, Pierce appealed to both the school board and the principal—brandishing James Youngblood's 1881 school law promising all children access to any public school.[42] Despite the law's threat of imprisonment or fine for violators, both entities denied his attempt. With no option left, Pierce sought legal counsel from a lawyer in Hightstown, New Jersey, named Adrian Symmes Appelget. An established lawyer, Appelget was also a veteran of the Civil War, serving twice in the Northern efforts against the South, first as a private in the New York Mounted

Adrian Symmes Appelget, photograph for GAR, n.d.

Rifles and subsequently as a Second Lieutenant in the New Jersey Cavalry, when he was captured and held as a prisoner of war.[43] After leaving the Army, he was elected Department Commander in the New Jersey Department of the Grand Army of the Republic (GAR), a fraternal organization for Union Army veterans.[44]

Through Appelget, Pierce attempted to seek judicial relief, illustrating his fortitude to exercise a right few

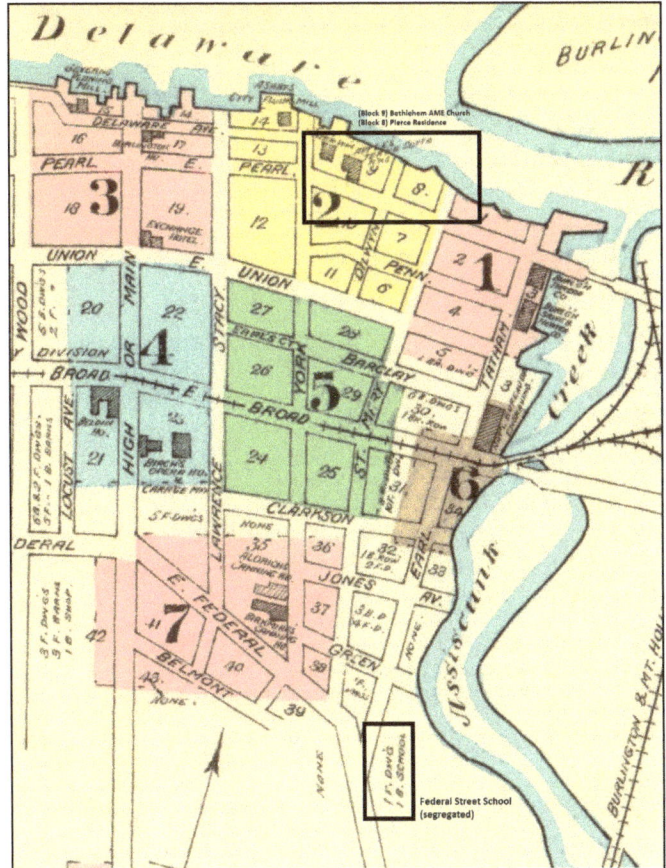

Detail, Sanborn Map Publishing Company, Burlington, Index Sheet, 1886.

black citizens retained the freedom to undertake. According to Gary Hunter in *Neighborhoods of Color*, African Americans rarely sought legal action because they could not afford lawyers and/or they did not want to lose their jobs, the inevitable consequence of fighting for civil rights during this era.[45] As an AME minister, however, Pierce knew that his consequences for seeking justice possessed few repercussions with church elders. Furthermore, the brevity of his preceding church appointments ensured he would be reappointed within a relatively short time, assuaging any long-term social consequences that might plague a permanent Burlington resident of color, who, after attempting action similar to Pierce, could endure a life rife with problems from those in opposition to his cause.

With this in mind, Pierce and Appelget filed their lawsuit on June 13, 1883, with the New Jersey Supreme Court. Morris H. Stratton, a member of the State Board of Education, served as lawyer for the Union District Trustees and the managers of Burlington's school fund.[46] The court heard the case on November 12, 1883, when Appelget laid out his case to attain a *writ of mandamus* (Lat. *we command*) from the Court, which would compel Burlington school officials to admit Pierce's children into the all-white schools.[47] Appelget's Brief of Counsel argues for the *writ of mandamus* on the following grounds:

> That the discrimination or division based on race or color lines, as herein complained of, is repugnant to and forbidden by the letter and spirit of the fourteenth amendment to the constitution of the United States, our state constitution and statutes.
>
> ... In 1871, section 94 of our school law was adopted, using the words "all persons," not *all white persons* [all emphasis original]; in 1875 the amendment to the state constitution striking out the word "white," and in 1881 a supplement to the school law, constituting it as misdemeanor to exclude *any child* from *any public school* on account of color.[48]

In response to Appelget, Morris H. Stratton utilized a three-pronged defense of the respondents' case.

1) The Trustees are elected by the public to manage the city's school system. This sovereignty permits the trustees to enact all laws not antithetical to the federal and state's extant laws, including discretionary decisions like a student's school placement.[49]
2) It is in the best interest of both classes to provide equal educational facilities in different places, as it provides black children the opportunity to learn from black teachers, and black teachers the opportunity to obtain gainful employment, as they would be "without place, occupation, or opportunity of usefulness in any mixed school...."[50]
3) The 1881 statute only enumerates "religion, nationality, or color" as reasons for inclusion, and the trustees denied Pierce's children on grounds of race, not color. In other words, "under the rule of the trustees, an Italian (for example) as dark as the relator's children would have been admitted, the exclusion was therefore, not to 'color,' but to race, which the statute does not prohibit."[51]

The court listened to both arguments, and reserved their decision for a later date. Local newspapers from New Jersey and Pennsylvania like *The Trenton Times*, *Bridgeton Evening News* and national newspapers like *The New-York Times* latched onto the trial—calling it "an interesting case" between "a colored preacher named Pierce" and the "trustees of union school district of Burlington."[52] Certain newspapers, like *The Trenton Times*, chose to ignore the racial aspect of the case. Instead, these papers reported that Pierce chose not to send his children to the Federal Street School because it was "700 paces farther away than any other school."[53]

On the first day of the Supreme Court's term, February 21, 1884, the court decided in Pierce's favor, ordering a *writ of mandamus* to the Union District Trustees. In the Court's opinion, they decided that the 1881 statute is unmistakably explicit, and the trustees' refusal to admit the children is therefore illegal, concluding, "... the children were entitled to admission, and, according to the proof, their exclusion was because the relator was a mulatto, or it was without any reason at all. In either case, it was unlawful."[54]

With the case won, a second round of newspaper coverage entered the press, this time containing divergent opinions on the case. *The Christian Reporter*, not surprisingly, lauded Pierce in his "victory over the prejudiced school board of his town," and even encouraged readers to help provide funds to defray his legal fees.[55] *The Trenton Times* recorded that the trial "created a sensation," while an editorial in the *Camden Daily Courier* sarcastically assailed the Union District Trustees by suggesting, "In the meantime, why not demand of the Almighty Father the setting aside a part of the domain of heaven for the especial use of the (here) colored people."[56]

Due to racial attitudes, certain newspapers decried the Court's decision. One Jersey City newspaper, *The Evening Journal*, recounted,

> The wildest kinds of plots for ousting these children are talked of. Many parents

declare the school system will be seriously affected. One opponent of Pierce, it is said, declared his willingness to head a party to burn the school house in which the colored children are to be admitted.[57]

The opponents' threat was not hollow: the Fair Haven School that instigated the 1881 law "mysteriously" burned to the ground only three years prior.[58] Like those in the community who opposed the decision, the Union School District Trustees also dissented from the court's action. In 1885, the trustees filed an appeal with the New Jersey Court of Errors and Appeals, only to have the court confirm the prior judgment.[59] Once and for all, this settled Pierce's victory. Editorials in the local papers captured some positive reaction from the community, including a newfound concern for the wellbeing of the students at the Federal Street School.[60] When reports appeared in the paper that the school board did not allocate enough resources for black children to learn to write, a so-called "pen and ink" crisis erupted. Editorials from concerned citizens asked; "If old enough to use the ordinary implements of writing, why upon earth should not the colored child have the same advantages as the white?" Another stated, "Let them have the pen and ink. I for one will help contribute the requisite, if any are too poor to buy."[61]

Undoubtedly, the "pen and ink" crisis tackled one of Pierce's major dilemmas: providing a proper education for the city's black students. However it failed to address his foremost concern: school segregation. While Pierce's four children attended the Stacy and St. Mary Schools in Burlington City, what happened to the other fifty black students attending the Federal Street School?

BLACK EDUCATION IN BURLINGTON COUNTY POST *PIERCE*

Although the *Pierce* case declared that no school official could exclude a child from a public school based on race, almost no changes occurred in the State's public school system. As is evident in Burlington County, instead of launching into the integration process, school officials doubled down on efforts to maintain segregation. Only a year after Pierce's victory, Reverend J. H. Accooe, a known acquaintance of Pierce, underwent hostility from his own congregation when he attempted and failed to send his children to Mount Holly Township's public school designated for white children.[62]

The next blow to the *Pierce* decision arrived in 1896, when the federal Supreme Court ruled in *Plessy v. Ferguson* that public facilities could be segregated, so long as facilities offered to white citizens equaled those offered to black citizens. The *Plessy* decision immediately vacated any opportunity for *Pierce* to impact the legal system. In 1899, a black woman named Elizabeth Cisco tested *Plessy* by filing a lawsuit against the School Board in Queens, New York, to send her children to a local all-white school. Though she cited the *Pierce* case, the court denied her request for a mandamus, stating, "We find nothing in the Constitution which deprived the school board of the proper management of the schools in its charge, or from determining where different classes of pupils should be educated, always providing, however, that the accommodations and facilities were equal for all."[63] In Burlington City, the case was no better. In 1903, Burlington's all-white high school refused to admit two female black students.[64] Due to *Plessy*, segregation expanded throughout Burlington County.

A statistical comparison between 1900 and 1915 offers further insight into the expansion of school segregation. This period was chosen for three reasons: 1900 and 1915 are both in the "Post-*Pierce*" and "Post-*Plessy*" era. Both years contain complete census records and near-complete data on "colored students" in the Superintendent's Report, and this period saw more black schools erected than any other period of time up to that date in Burlington County history. The statistics from this period demonstrate that between 1900 and 1915, the state's population increased by 51%, totaling 2.8 million people.[65] During the same time frame, Burlington County's population increased by 28.3%, totaling 74,737 residents.[66] Statistics from the Superintendent reports indicate that the aggregate number of black students in Burlington County actually decreased by 25.9%, totaling 478 students.[67]

Table 2 illustrates a data matrix of known black schools operating in Burlington County in 1915. The eight variables listed in column two, "School Name," indicate that the county facilitated eight schools educating 478 black students. One of the table's salient features appears in column three, "Established Date." With the exception of Bordentown, each school was built after 1900. If this data set expanded its temporal periodization into the following decade, it would indicate a continuing trend of new segregated schools. For example, in Mount Laurel, New Jersey, town officials constructed "School No. 3" in 1918 for the sole purpose of educating black children.[68]

This data trend indicates that in the post-*Plessy* era, local leaders in South Jersey made an effort to double-down on school segregation, which the federal Supreme Court permitted. The trend grows even more apparent when comparing Table 2 with population statistics. As previously stated, the total population of Burlington County increased 28.3% between 1900 and 1915, while the number of black students decreased by 25.9%. Therefore, as the population increased and the total number of black students decreased, it would seem likely that local officials would consolidate black

Table 2

Operational Black Schools in Burlington County, 1915		
Municipality	**School Name**	**Established Date**
Bordentown	Elementary School No. 2	1853
	Manual Training and Industrial School for Colored Youth	1886
Burlington	William R. Allen	1900
Cinnaminson	Five Points School	1906
Delran	Bridgeboro or Aronson Bell School	1907
Evesham	Milford School	Pre-1915
Moorestown	Moorestown Public School No. 7	1915
Mount Holly	Samuel Aaron School	1908
Source: Louis Kaser, *A Story of the Public Schools of Burlington County* (Riverton, NJ: Press of the New Era, 1943).		

and white schools. As the data in Table 2 illustrates, however, school officials continued to construct new black schools for a decreasing student body.[69] This indicates a resolute effort by school officials to entrench segregation in Burlington County, suggesting a pedagogy promoting a "separate, but equal" education. Therefore, it makes sense that, in 1904, Burlington City's supervising principal transferred all eight black children attending the city's white schools back to the newly erected William R. Allen School, a segregated facility. By analyzing the data presented in Table 2, in conjunction with population statistics, it becomes apparent that Burlington County and the State of New Jersey ignored the progressive *Pierce* decision, and instead continued the systematic segregation prevalent between 1900 and 1915.

Disparate Views on Education

The fact that school officials continued to build segregated schools for a decreasing black student population raises questions pertaining to the officials' justification for such an endeavor. During this period, however, the educational pedagogy of Booker T. Washington, who served as the leading spokesman and organizer of black citizens, dominated the realm of African American education. Unlike Pierce, Washington did not believe in organizing black citizens against segregation, discrimination, and civil rights violations, but, instead, believed "that through financial successes and by making themselves indispensable to the South's economic growth, eventually African-Americans would earn their way into full citizenship...."[70] Unfortunately for Pierce, Washington's pedagogy flew in the face of his goals.

Booker T. Washington believed that a student's learning should provide him or her with skills necessary for employment. In 1881, Washington founded the Tuskegee Institute in Tuskegee, Alabama, a sprawling school designed to improve educational standards for black children living in Alabama. Washington contended that education would improve the social standing of black individuals in the South, making them "so much more useful in his labour, so much better a citizen, and so much more dependable in all the relations of life...."[71] However, not just any education would do. Washington instead believed in the utility of industrialized education.[72] As he writes,

> The mere fact that a boy has learned in school to handle a plane or that he has learned something about the chemistry of the soil does not of itself insure that he has gained any new and vital grip upon the life about him. He must at the same time learn to use the knowledge and the training he has received to change and improve the conditions about him.[73]

Although initially intended for southern states, Washington's popularity promulgated the concept of industrial education throughout the north, including New Jersey. In 1886, Reverend W. A. Rice, an AME minister in the New Jersey Annual Conference, established a vocational school for black children based on Washington's pedagogy. Erected in Bordentown, New Jersey, the Ironside Normal School served as a vocational school for black students in New Jersey, teaching agriculture, wood-working, general mechanics, domestic science, beauty culture, dressmaking, and, later, automobile mechanics.[74] Over the following decades, the school reported valiant progress and attained support from those in New Jersey and the AME church at large. An 1898 article in *The Christian Recorder* promotes the school's widespread support: "The school has always advanced, but during the past two or three years its progress has been phenomenal. It is conducted along lines similar to those upon which the Tuskegee School is operated, and the results, thus far, give promise of much greater results in the future."[75]

As Washington promoted industrialized education, he gained a rival. During the early 1900s, W. E. B. Du Bois dissented from the idea of separate vocational education. To Du Bois, focusing on vocational education forced students to accept an inferior position in relation to white people. He believed that the best means to integrate into society was to prove the intellectual capabilities of the black race, something that rote, industrialized tasks failed to do. For Du Bois, there was a difference between *earning a living* and *making a living*. In a 1906 speech at Hampton Institute, a pro-Washington school, Du Bois assailed the leaders of the school for influencing students not to "hitch their wagons to a star but to hitch them to a mule."[76] As Du Bois biographer David Levering Lewis concludes, Du Bois was alarmed by the thought of a future generation who only knew "the handicapping of intellectual ambition, the inculcation of civic timidity, and the rationalization of second-best as the best possible for them."[77]

Like Du Bois, Pierce disagreed with the idea of a generation taught separate from their white counterparts. However, the AME church in New Jersey held an unclear stance on education. Certain members of the AME denomination followed Washington and Rice by supporting segregated, industrialized education. For example, parishioners from Mount Moriah AME church in Mount Holly prohibited their minister, Reverend J. H. Accooe, from sending his children to the white school in 1885. Before he could file a lawsuit, church laity distributed a resolution supporting the black school.[78] Moreover, Reverend Rice's Ironside School in Bordentown completely diverged from what Pierce had attempted to accomplish.

With such an obscured platform, Jeremiah Pierce led a charge to explicitly define the church's attitude towards education at the New Jersey AME Church Annual Conference in 1892. After a report from Reverend Rice, Pierce and a cadre of ministers expressed their desire to disassociate the AME church from Reverend Rice and the Ironside School. According to the published Annual Conference Minutes, Pierce wrote a resolution stating, "That we, the members of the New Jersey Annual Conference, denounce *in toto* the action of Rev. W. A. S. Rice in the course he has taken in his pretension to an industrial school," and that "the said Rev. Rice is hereby warned against the attempt to use in any way the title of the African Methodist Episcopal Church, as he has been doing in the past." Pierce further criticized the school, calling it a "pretend enterprise."[79]

Unfortunately for Pierce, most individuals followed Washington's concept of accommodation and non-agitation.[80] By 1900, the Ironside School at Bordentown received praise from the majority in the AME church. In a June 7, 1900, article annotating the school's graduation, *The Christian Recorder* comments:

> In a general way the progress made by this enterprise is to be commended. It was started as a private enterprise by Rev. W. A. Rice, who was at one time connected with the New Jersey Conference of our Church. It has since passed under the management of the State Board of Education and will in future receive substantial aid from the State.
>
> It is doing a good and great work. The [graduation] exercises on Friday last proved, beyond doubt, that its growth has been a healthy one.[81]

Washington's ideology largely went untouched until August 1908, when severe riots between white and black citizens in Springfield, Illinois, launched race relations into the forefront of the nation's consciousness. William English Walling, a well-known socialist and politician, famously wrote in *The Independent* that, "... the spirit of the abolitionists, of Lincoln and of Lovejoy, must be revived and we must come to treat the negro on a plane of absolute political and social equality." He then asked, "... who realizes the seriousness of the situation, and what large and powerful body of citizens is ready to come to their aid?"[82] This call triggered the National Negro Convention in New York City and the eventual birth of the National Association for the Advancement of Colored People (NAACP). According to Du Bois biographer David L. Lewis, the creation of the NAACP:

> ... marked the end of the era of accommodation, the twilight of ... Washington, Du Bois wrote. "The answer long forced on the American world has been: let them alone, do not agitate, do not let loose dangerous forces and passions," he thundered in *Survey*. Now the passions were loose. The problem of the twentieth century was about to be attacked, vigorously and collectively.[83]

Had Pierce possessed support from an organization like the NAACP, which would eventually help integrate Burlington's schools in 1948, one wonders whether his court decision would have made more of an impact in New Jersey.

Comprehending Pierce's Legacy

In 1884, Jeremiah Pierce published a 52-page monograph documenting his State Supreme Court case. The work contains a brief autobiography, the arguments of the relator and respondent, and editorials that appeared in local papers responding to his victory. In his text, Pierce provides three explanations for his fight against school segregation:

> In the FIRST place, I desire to show that public sentiment is one thing, and law is another.
>
> SECOND, to show the importance of standing up for our rights as citizens.
>
> THIRD, to inspire my race to take a proper and loyal course through life, and to learn never to be found leaning upon others when you can as well stand alone.[84]

While Pierce believed that his role as a father required him to seek the best possible opportunity for his children to learn, the text above illustrates that he ultimately believed that as he fought for his children's right to a quality education, he was also confronting something much larger: the inadequate state of black schools plaguing New Jersey during the post-civil war era. When Pierce writes that he wants to remind others of his race of "the importance of standing up for our rights as citizens," he has a specific group of citizens in mind. Undoubtedly, he is urging black citizens to fight for their right to attain an adequate education. When he states that he wants to "inspire my race," he reflects his desire not just to inspire his children, but also to see all black people given the chance to receive a quality education.[85]

Pierce's case illustrates that even if a person of color could confront segregation by securing a victory in his state's highest court during the post-civil war era, the legal, institutional, and organizational support required to act upon such a victory did not exist. Even in 1948, Burlington City only desegregated their schools by eliciting help from the NAACP, a Citizens Committee, the school superintendent and the city's school board. Despite Pierce's most adamant opposition, he was only a single individual fighting against an ideology that urged black citizens not to agitate against the *status quo*, but instead to rely on segregated, vocational-style education as a way to achieve economic independence. Pierce, and later Du Bois, found this ideology to be the root cause of black citizens' oppression.[86] As Pierce explains, the only way to combat this subjugation is through academic training and the judicial system:

> The laws of this country have been made plain to defend every citizen in his rights, but for want of moral courage, O how many fall back and allow themselves to be deprived of that which would do them good and add greatly to their comfort—I mean their God-given rights.[87]

Unfortunately for Pierce, civil rights cases often failed to succeed without support from legal, institutional, and organizational backing on a national scale. The little momentum he rallied came to a crashing halt twelve years later, when the federal Supreme Court declared the constitutionality of the "separate-but-equal" doctrine in *Plessy v Ferguson*. Although *Plessy* left Pierce's lawsuit a mere personal victory for himself and his children, his action should be remembered as one of the countless battles fought in the war to end school segregation during the post-Civil War era.

Endnotes

Zachary Baer is a senior at Rowan University, working to obtain a BA in Secondary Education and History. He is a member of the West Jersey History Roundtable and holds a deep, abiding interest in local history and the history of education and race. Zachary resides in Gibbsboro, New Jersey, and looks forward to receiving feedback and comments from *SoJourn* readers. Comments can be sent directly to the author at zacharytbaer@gmail.com.

This research project and culminating article would not have been possible without the support of his family and friends. Most especially, he would like to thank Paul W. Schopp, who provided unremitting guidance, assistance, and support throughout every stage of this project.

1. "Burlington Acts to Eliminate Segregation in Public Schools," *Sunday Times-Advertiser* (Trenton, NJ), June 6, 1948, 8.
2. Robert Korstad and Nelson Lichtenstein, "Opportunities found and Lost: Labor, Radicals, and the Early Civil Rights Movement," *The Journal of American History* 75, 3 (1988): 787.
3. Linton Satterthwait, "The Color-Line in New Jersey," in *The Arena*, ed. B. O. Flower (Boston, MA: Albert Brandt, 1906), 394-400; Marion Manola Wright, *The Education of Negroes in New Jersey* (New York: Teachers College, 1941), 173; Clement A. Price, *Freedom Not Far Distant: A Documentary History of Afro-Americans in New Jersey* (Newark, NJ: New Jersey Historical Society, 1980), 143-50; Ernest Lyght, *Path of Freedom: The Black Presence in New Jersey's Burlington County 1659 – 1900* (Cherry Hill, NJ: E. & E. Publishing House, 1978), 85-86; Gary J. Hunter, *Neighborhoods of Color: African American Communities in Southern New Jersey, 1638 – 2000* (Glassboro, NJ: Neighborhoods of Color Committee, 2015), 53; Robert L. Thompson, *Burlington Biographies: A History of Burlington, New Jersey, Told Through the Lives and Times of Its People* (Galloway, NJ: South Jersey Culture & History Center, 2016).
4. The "Allen School" denotes the name of the all black school in Burlington; Lyght, *Path of Freedom*, 86.
5. "'Good Old Days' Weren't So Good," *Asbury Park Press*, August 29, 1982, C6; Price, *Freedom Not Far Distant*, 143.

6 New Jersey Constitution (1844), article VII, pt. VI.
7 Nelson Burr, *Education in New Jersey 1630 – 1871* (Princeton, NJ: Princeton University Press, 1942), 266.
8 *Annual Report of the Superintendents of Public Schools* (Trenton, NJ: Sherman and Harron, 1847), 3-11.
9 Burr, *Education*, 156.
10 *Annual Report of the Superintendents of Public Schools* (Trenton, NJ: Phillips & Boswell, 1850), 23.
11 State lawmakers split Chester Township in 1860, erecting Cinnaminson Township out of Chester's northern half. While census records acknowledge Cinnaminson, the Superintendent's report keeps Cinnaminson in Chester; John F. Snyder, *The Story of New Jersey's Civil Boundaries 1606 – 1968* (Trenton, NJ: Bureau of Geology and Topography, 1969), 94.
12 James Still, *Early Recollections and Life of Dr. James Still*, 1877. Reprint (Galloway, NJ: South Jersey Culture & History Center, 2015), 8.
13 M. H. Stratton writes in his Counsel for Respondents that, "It is only where the special circumstances of the case justify the increased expense, that special schools are provided for the special class … as in cities as large as Burlington." This indicates that at least in South Jersey, where large black populations existed, officials created schools for their educational accommodation; Jeremiah H. Pierce, *Brief Statement of Public School Contest* (Philadelphia: Christian Recorder, 1884), 25.
14 Burr, *Education*, 281.
15 *Acts of the Ninety-Eighth Legislature of the State of New Jersey* (Paterson, NJ: Chiswell & Wurts, 1874), 135.
16 *Annual Report of the State Board of Education and Superintendent of Public Instruction* (Trenton, NJ: 1870), 187; *Annual Report of the State Board of Education* (Trenton, NJ: 1880), 129.
17 *Annual Report*, 1870, 191; *Annual Report*, 1880, 113.
18 Thompson, *Burlington Biographies*, 345.
19 Ibid., 346.
20 Burlington County Deed Book K-8, pg. 636, *et seq.*; Burlington County Deed Book G-8, pg. 222, *et seq.*; Burlington County Deed Book K-8, pg. 638.
21 "State Items," *Daily State Gazette* (Trenton, NJ), February 26, 1881.
22 "The School Trouble at Fair Haven," *The Evening Journal*, March 1, 1881.
23 "State Items," *Daily State Gazette* (Trenton, NJ), March 17, 1881.
24 "The Color Line," *The Evening Journal* (Jersey City, NJ), March 8, 1881; *Acts of the One Hundred and Fifth Legislature of the State of New Jersey* (Gloucester City, NJ: Thomas C. Hamilton, 1881), 186; Wright, *Education of Negroes*, 167.
25 "Passage of the Educational Bill," *The Sentinel* (Trenton, NJ), March 19, 1881.
26 Hunter, *Neighborhoods*, 52.
27 1850 United States Census, Bridgeton, Cumberland County, New Jersey, digital image s.v. "Jeremiah Pierce," http://www.Ancestry.com.
28 William Steward and Theophilus G. Steward, *Gouldtown: A Very Remarkable Settlement of Ancient Date* (Philadelphia, PA: J. B. Lippincott Company, 1913), 51.
29 1850 Census. Mulatto is a term used to denote a person of mixed white and black ancestry.
30 Steward, *Gouldtown*, 50.
31 "Acknowledgements," *The Christian Recorder*, December 28, 1861.
32 Marriage Records, New Jersey State Archives, Book H, Page 493.
33 Pierce, *Brief Statement*, III.
34 Ibid.
35 Pierce, *Brief Statement*, III.
36 Ibid., IV.
37 Ibid.
38 "Colored Children in the Public Schools," in *The New Jersey Law Journal*, ed. Edward Q. Keasbey et al. (Somerville, NJ: Honeyman & Company, 1883), 286.
39 Pierce, *Brief Statement*, 49.
40 Ibid., 49.
41 Ibid., 2.
42 *Acts of the One Hundred and Fifth Legislature of the State of New Jersey* (Gloucester City, NJ: Thomas C. Hamilton, 1881), 186.
43 Pierce, *Brief Statement*, V; "Appelget Once Fled Bloodhounds," *Trenton Evening Times*, November 6, 1909, 3.
44 Organization Index to Pension Files of Veterans Who Served Between 1861 and 1900, New Jersey, digital image s.v. "Adrian Appelget," *Fold3.com*.; "Bloodhounds," *Trenton Evening Times*, 1909.
45 Hunter, *Neighborhoods*, 52.
46 Pierce, *Brief Statement*, 19; C. H. Evans, *American College and Public School Directory*, vol. 5 (Missouri: C. H. Evans & Co., 1883), np.
47 Henry Campbell Black, *Black's Law Dictionary*, 6th edition (Minnesota: West Publishing Co., 1990), 961; Garret D. W. Vroom, *Reports of Cases Argued in the Supreme Court of the State of New Jersey* (Trenton, NJ: The W. S. Sharp Printing Company, 1885), 76.
48 Pierce, *Brief Statement*, 6-7.
49 Ibid., 21.
50 Ibid., 22.
51 Vroom, *Supreme Court*, 79.
52 "The Color Line in Schools," *Bridgeton Evening News* (Bridgeton, NJ), November 14, 1883, 3.
53 "The Color Line in Burlington," *The Trenton Times*, November 12, 1883.
54 Vroom, *Supreme Court*, 79.
55 "Rev. J. H. Pierce, of the Burlington Station," *The Christian Recorder*, March 20, 1884.
56 "State News in Brief," *Trenton Evening Times*, March 13, 1884; As quoted in: Pierce, *Brief Statement*, 44.
57 "The Color War in the Schools," *The Evening Journal* (Jersey City, NJ), March 7, 1884.
58 Wright, *Education of Negroes*, 164.
59 Union District Trustees v. State, Court of Errors and Appeals of New Jersey, 47 N.J.L. 348(S.C. NJ 1885) LexisNexis.
60 Pierce, *Brief Statement*, 51.
61 Ibid., 51.

62 "The Rev. J. H. Accooe is having a slight controversy in Mt Holly," *The Christian Recorder*, July 23, 1885; Rev. Accooe served as Pierce's predecessor in Allentown and refers to Pierce in Rev. J. H. Accooe, "Word From Allentown, NJ" *The Christian Recorder*, March 6, 1884.

63 Edmund H. Smith, Reports of Cases Decided in the Court of Appeals of the State of New York, Volume 161 (Albany, NY: James B. Lyon, 1900), 602.

64 Satterthwait, "Color-Line," 396.

65 Department of State, Census Bureau, *Compendium of Censuses 1726 – 1905, Together with the Tabulated Returns of 1905* (Trenton, NJ: J. L. Murphy Publishing Co., 1906), 76.

66 State Census Bureau, *Compendium*, 55.

67 *Annual Report of the Board of Education and of the Superintendent of Public Instruction of New Jersey* (Trenton, NJ: MacCrellish & Quigley, 1901), 148; *Annual Report of the State Board of Education of New Jersey* (Somerville, NJ: The Unionist-Gazette Association, 1916), 232.

68 Kaser, *Public Schools of Burlington*, 121.

69 Satterthwait, "Color-Line," 396.

70 David Levering Lewis, *W. E. B. Du Bois: Biography of Race 1868 – 1919* (New York: Owl Books, 1993), 240.

71 Booker T. Washington, *My Larger Education* (Garden City, NY: Doubleday Page & Company, 1911), 300.

72 Nina Mjagkij, *Organizing Black America: An Encyclopedia of African American Associations* (New York, NY: Garland Publishing, 2001), 659.

73 Washington, *Education*, 143.

74 Ironside later becomes the Manual Training and Industrial School for Colored Youth; Lyght, *Path of Freedom*, 84; The New Jersey Conference of Social Work, *The Negro in New Jersey* (Newark, NJ: The Department of Institutions and Agencies, 1932), 40.

75 "The 'Ironside' Commencement," *The Christian Recorder*, June 23, 1898.

76 Lewis, *Du Bois*, 353.

77 Ibid.

78 Lyght, *Path of Freedom*, 86.

79 *Journal of the Twentieth Session After Organization of the New Jersey Annual Conference of the African Methodist Episcopal Church Held at Morristown, N.J. from April 20th to 26th* (Atlanta, GA: Franklin Printing House, 1892), 20-22.

80 Lewis, *Du Bois*, 398.

81 "The 'Ironsides' [*sic*] Commencement," *The Christian Recorder*, June 7, 1900.

82 Lewis, *Du Bois*, 388-9.

83 Ibid., 398.

84 Pierce, *Brief Statement*, n.p.

85 Pierce, *Brief Statement*, V.

86 Lewis, *Du Bois*, 244-45.

87 Pierce, *Brief Statement*, V.

Most visitors to Atlantic City arrived to enjoy the beach, the boardwalk and the salt air. For those seeking to remain "far from the maddening crowd," the allure of the back bay and its recreational activities, ranging from fishing and crabbing to boating, caused some to build boathouses along various channels in the meadowlands. This particular boathouse, complete with a small marine railway to pull a craft from the water, was likely located on the south shore of Clam Creek, a small channel extending between the entrance of Gardner's Basin and the entrance to Bucks Basin at the north end of Absecon Island.

Where Blackberries Grew:
Margaret Mead in Hammonton

Patricia Chappine and Mark Demitroff

The Town of Hammonton, a flourishing Pinelands community, boasts an intriguing cultural heritage—one built on the perseverance of waves of immigrants who forged farming communities on supposedly infertile land.[1] It is nestled in the Pinelands National Reserve, a seemingly endless sandy plain of meandering streams and tatty pine/oak woodlands. Legend has an Irishman named Mullen as the first settler here; he kept a tavern in his cabin at the head of Hammonton Lake.[2] Historically, we know William Coffin Sr. and Jonathan Haines built a window glassworks here in 1817, the former's son John Hammond Coffin being Old Hammonton's namesake.[3] But it was real estate speculators Charles K. Landis and Richard J. Byrnes whose land scheme of New Hammonton ultimately tamed the unbroken wilderness along a new rail service, midway on the line between Philadelphia and Atlantic City. A wide swath was slashed along the new tracks and marginal farmland was parceled out to earnest home-seekers wishing to grow market gardens on small plots, all framed in agrarian bliss.[4] Cheap land and rail transportation turned pine wilderness into what would become an "ethnic archipelago."[5, 6]

Here is where the story gets interesting, as the town and its inhabitants did not go unnoticed by the outside world. In fact, this introduction prepares the ground for the remarkable career of a woman, whose outspoken and, at times, controversial intellect has forever changed the way we perceive our surroundings. Renowned ethnographer Margaret Mead spent a portion of her early years living in Hammonton's Little Italy neighborhood while her mother, Emily Fogg Meade, endeavored to study the lives of the Italian immigrants there.[7, 8] The story of the Meades' short stay in an ethnic settlement in the New Jersey "frontier" and the paradigm-changing ethnographic work that resulted is a little known, yet essential part of southern New Jersey history.[9]

Born in 1901, Margaret Mead was arguably the most celebrated anthropologist of the twentieth century. Her notoriety began with the best-selling book *Coming of Age in Samoa* (1928). Scholars have reacted to this ethnography with both support and condemnation in the decades since its initial release. Her second book, *Growing up in New Guinea* (1930), further propelled her into public discourse. Her visibility, through a variety of media, made her an easily identifiable figure throughout her life.[10] While many people are familiar with her work on Samoa

Margaret Mead in 1948. *From the Smithsonian Institute Archives.*

and New Guinea, she also gained recognition for her critiques of American society and culture.[11] Importantly, Margaret embodied what is now commonly called "public anthropology," which is activist in nature and seeks to "apply anthropological methods . . . to issues of concern to a wide range of social sectors," essentially making this genre more accessible to the public.[12] Her influential role in the development of systems analysis and cybernetics helped to develop and explain complex systems theory, which, in part, has been the basis for computer software today.[13]

In her role as a prominent anthropologist and cultural commentator, Margaret brought issues of gender and academics to the foreground. She was acclaimed as a symbol of the "New Woman" by some and criticized by others, notably Betty Friedan,[14] for stressing a woman's role as that of wife and mother in her book *Male and Female* (1949).[15] In actuality, Margaret herself broke traditional gender roles at an early age. In *Blackberry Winter: My Earlier Years* (1972), she said her father once remarked, "It's a pity you aren't a boy, you'd have gone far."[16] Mother dressed "Punk"—as she was called—in sensible bloomers instead of petticoats to allow her "young daughter to climb the tallest pine."[17] The idea of gender discrimination continued to impact her throughout her life. Before she left for fieldwork in Samoa, she wrote a poem about the limits of being born a female in the early twentieth century:

> Measure your thread and cut it
> To suit your little seam,
> Stitch the garment tightly, tightly,
> And leave no room for dream.[18]

Margaret Mead self-portrait completed around the age of thirteen, ca. 1914 – 1915. *Pastel on paper, from the Library of Congress Manuscript Division.*

Despite the many crucibles Margaret faced, she completed years of successful fieldwork both in the United States and abroad, becoming a leading figure in anthropology, a discipline that was then overwhelmingly male-dominated.

As a child of the Progressive Era,[19] Margaret was a staunch proponent of using the social sciences to improve civilization. She was among a small faction of academics who did not subscribe to the popular notion of genetics as an explanation for low scores on intelligence tests. According to Elizabeth Messina, a psychologist and author, Margaret was one of the few "Active academic social scientists, anthropologists, and psychologists" who "argued that racial differences did not, on face value, constitute evidence for a genetic interpretation of racial differences in IQ."[20] In the early part of the twentieth century, many immigrant groups, Italians among them, faced prejudice and discrimination in the United States. This animus was also deep-seated against Hammonton's southern Italian and Sicilian farm community as expressed in a federal report, stating that "these people belong to the much-maligned . . . most problematic, if not the most undesirable, of the south European group."[21] According to David Richards, a professor of criminal law, "The force of American racism fell with all its accustomed ferocity on the recent immigrants, making them ideological scapegoats."[22] Margaret was one of the few who sought to change these now-discredited ideas.

Much of this anti-immigrant fervor was supported by a new pseudoscience called "eugenics," first introduced in 1883 by Sir Francis Galton, a half-cousin of Charles Darwin. Derived from a Greek word meaning "well born," eugenics conveyed the belief that heredity, not education or opportunity, determined a person's intelligence and capacity to contribute to the community. Galton and his contemporaries believed positive traits could be promoted and negative traits could be eliminated from society.[23] Advocates of eugenics believed in the natural inferiority of certain races falsely stigmatized by eugenicists, maligning newcomers such as Hammonton's emigrants.[24] The large influx of Italians can be traced back to the growing season of 1877, when they became the settlement's favored farm labor pool, since that year the Germans failed to show up in significant numbers.[25] Scarcity of resources and jobs, whether real or imagined, often led to outcries against unbridled immigration of new emigrant groups. According to social scientists, "stigmatization is a universal and socially defined feature of human life."[26] While the target groups changed over time, the tendency towards prejudicial attitudes remained. With the influx of new groups and the rapid social changes brought on by industrialization, many Americans refocused their own anxieties outward, finding convenient targets in immigrant populations.[27]

During the first few decades of the twentieth century, some social scientists used biased intelligence testing to stigmatize immigrants. However, Margaret was committed to finding evidence to the contrary. Her studies on the children of Italian immigrants in Hammonton proved intelligence testing was biased and unreliable. Her work found the amount of English spoken at home, along with the time the family had lived in the United States, all contributed to increased scores. Thus, she concluded that the idea of a primarily genetic basis for intelligence was patently false. In her quest for social justice, Mead went against the rising tide of academia by drawing attention to the inequities of both the intelligence testing and the treatment of Italian children in the American school system.[28]

Margaret, however, was not the only social crusader in her family. Her fieldwork was an expansion of her mother's earlier ethnographic work on Italian immigrants in Hammonton. In 1902, a year after Margaret's birth, Emily Fogg Meade first arrived at this small town to begin a doctoral dissertation, which she never completed. Her master's study was published in a report titled *The Italian on the Land* (1907), submitted to the United States Department of Labor. It was Margaret's grandmother, Martha Adaline Ramsay Meade, who purchased a home for the family in Hammonton on August 19, 1903.[29] Martha Meade grew up in Winchester, Ohio, and was, at the time of the acquisition, a widowed schoolteacher who lived with her lone child—Edward Sherwood Meade, Margaret's father.[30] The Meades were originally Yankees with deep family roots going back to the Puritans,[31] being the same blue-blood American stock that Landis and Byrnes courted to establish New Hammonton a half-century earlier.

As ever-increasing numbers of European immigrants flocked to the United States for opportunities, government officials began to question whether or not further restrictions on entrance should be applied. In response to this, Emily endeavored to find examples of successful immigrant populations. She writes:

> It is alleged that they are underfed, ill grown, often diseased, unskilled, illiterate, quiescent, lacking in responsibility, with a keen sense of inferiority and the lack of the ability to take advantage of new circumstances; that their standard of living is low, and that they do not improve it when they prosper; above all, that they are likely to become public charges in hospitals, insane asylums, or almshouses.[32]

Conversely, Emily's study finds these views to be largely the product of an uninformed public, fearful of their own economic situation and lashing out, with native-born prejudices, at immigration as a source of their distress. Of Italian immigrants in particular, she states, "they are naturally gregarious and seek their own people who can speak their language."[33] In her own words, Emily chose Hammonton for her study because "the increase of the Italian population in that section has been natural, it has not been stimulated or assisted in any way by Americans, and the immigrant has been thrown upon his own resources."[34] For her, the town represented a unique assimilation, where Italians and Americans "have grown up together."[35] She presents the town as an archetype of accomplishment, writing,

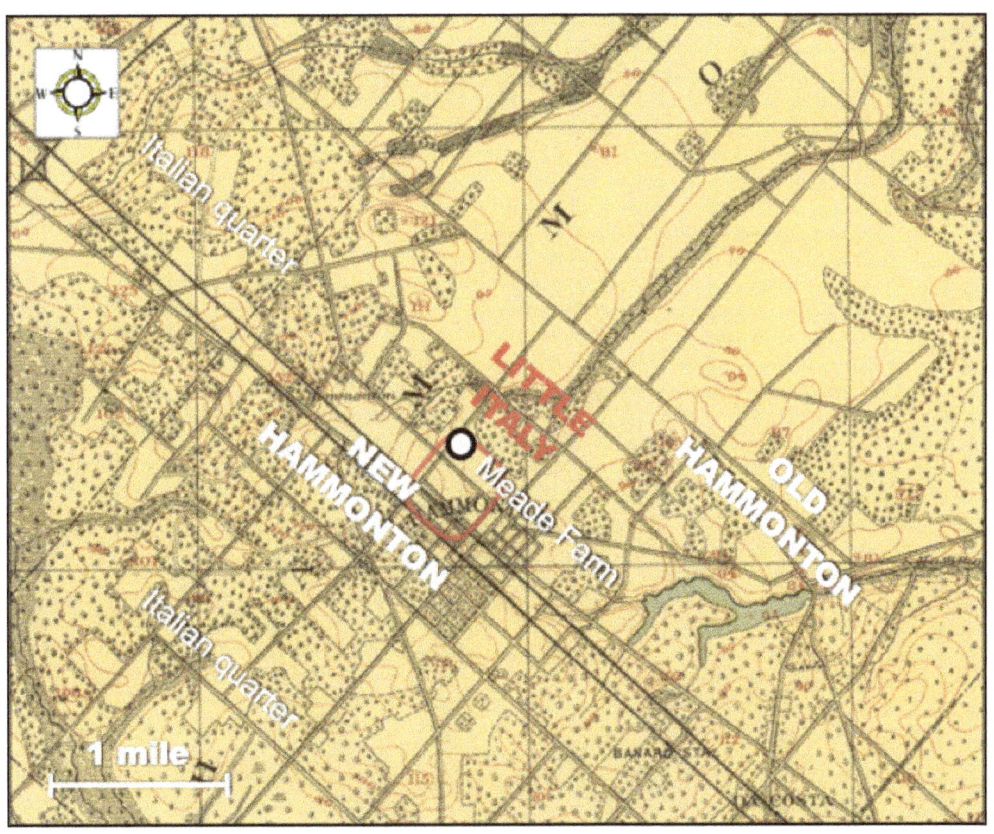

Map indicating the location of Hammonton before ("Old") and after ("New") railroad-spurred development by Landis & Byrnes. The approximate area of the segregated "Italian quarter" as per Dillingham (1911). "Little Italy" neighborhood is outlined in red (Personal Communication, Gabriel Donio, August 31, 2016). A bullet marks Meade's Six-Acre lot. Forest area and tree density can be inferred by icons. Cultivated area is designated by the absence of tree icons. Adapted from Cook & Vermeule (1887: Sheet 15).

"What the Italian has been able to accomplish in Hammonton he can achieve elsewhere under similar circumstances."[36] She goes on to note, "If it had not been for the Italian settlers the vicinity of Hammonton might still be wilderness."[37] Early Italian immigrants cleared land and set up farms in the emptiness of the Pine Barrens, slowly building the town and making it, according to Emily, "one of the most attractive spots in the pine region of southern New Jersey."[38] Her work presents the story of Italian immigrants who built lives for themselves and subsequent generations through hard work, frugality, ingenuity and perseverance, qualities that built the town of Hammonton. This was accomplished "on some of the poorest and sandiest soils in south Jersey," these newcomers creating "a real oasis in a waste of sand and lowland."[39] Regarding social relations, she believed the traits of Italian families should be exalted and emulated by others, stating, "Family bonds are strong, and social pleasures are enjoyed by the family as a whole. Italians not only value children for their labor, but they have great affection for them and are uniformly kind to them. To have many children is considered a blessing."[40]

Because of Emily's research logistics, the family moved about four times a year, usually residing in Hammonton during the spring and fall to fit the seasonal rhythms of planting and harvesting. Margaret developed a deep sense of attachment to the town, writing, "All other houses were strange-houses that had to be made our own as quickly as possible so that they no longer would be strange."[41] According to Margaret, "We had five whole acres, a good part of which was second-growth bush, studded with blueberries . . . However far away we moved and however often, we always came home again to Hammonton and the familiar and loved things that were too fragile to take with us."[42, 43]

Margaret's father, Edward Sherwood Meade, was an economics professor at the Wharton School of Finance and Economy. His academic institution, unlike other American colleges, employed German teaching philosophy that encouraged academic freedom and valued seminar and practical field study over lecture and recitation.[44, 45] Professor Meade urged industry promoters to venture into untried fields,[46] "whose success will increase the wealth of the community" by exploiting wasted mineral resources like water for

The Meade family home in Hammonton, 1908. *Courtesy of the Paul W. Schopp Collection.*

power and irrigation.[47] Meade concomitantly had vested commodity-based business interests, including recycling of public water supplies.[48] It is possible that the Hammonton move harbored another agenda, to facilitate water and agricultural pursuits on the adjoining Wharton Tract, where Joseph Wharton was actively pursuing a scheme to commoditize Pine Barrens water for public use through the widespread construction of reservoirs, although evidence does not yet support this conjecture.

While living in Hammonton, Margaret, the first of five children born to Emily and Edward, was home-schooled by Martha, who believed children benefited from learning the lessons of nature. Grandmother Meade was also a staunch proponent of the importance of learning practical skills and, to this end, Margaret became a student of the local culture and nature. She writes, "In Hammonton, there was a woman who was a magnificent woodcarver, so I learned woodcarving."[49] In her youth, Margaret displayed both a sense of compassion and pragmatism. In one account, her aunt came to visit the family on their farm and found a young Margaret crying over the death of several chickens, which the family had butchered for dinner. Her aunt recalled, "Her softness of heart was very touching, until she made it plain that it wasn't the killing of the chickens that disturbed her, as [much as] the fact that she hadn't been told about it."[50]

Despite this idyllic childhood, the Meades did not retain their home in Hammonton long. Reportedly the result of an affair carried on by Margaret's father, Edward, the family sold their Hammonton home in 1910 and moved to Bucks County, Pennsylvania.[51] By Margaret's recollection, her father nearly left the family entirely, but "after mother had established how much money she would need to bring us up properly, there wouldn't have been anything left."[52]

Margaret revisited her ties in Hammonton to work on a master's thesis titled "Intelligence Tests of Italian and American Children," which she completed for a degree in psychology from Columbia University in 1924. She concluded that the deciding factor in the higher performance of English-speaking children demonstrated culture, and not inborn abilities. According to Nancy Lutkehaus, a professor of anthropology at the University of Southern California, "Her findings were in opposition to those who wanted to use intelligence tests to argue the inferiority of Southern Europeans and Eastern European Jews in order to restrict their entry into the United States."[53] Margaret recognized the unfair impressions American society carried of new immigrants and blamed the sensational media for the proliferation of these stereotypes among the American public. In April 1923, like her mother before her, she set out to correct these false ideas. To find evidence of bias, she administered the Otis group intelligence tests to children in grades 6 – 10.[54] Upon seeing that the Italian children scored lower, she concluded that the language spoken at home and the length of time the family had resided in the United States directly influenced the test scores. She writes, "Classification of foreign children in schools where they have to compete with American children, on the basis of group intelligence test findings alone, is not a just evaluation of the child's innate capacity." Mead effectively demonstrated bias in testing and brought the problem to the public's attention.[55]

Following her 1925 fieldwork in Samoa, Margaret expanded her ethnographic interests to include other immigrant groups like the Jews, the Ukrainians, and other Eastern Europeans, working with the Office of War Information and Office of Strategic Services.[56] However, her experience in Hammonton continued to impact her throughout her life, as both a home during her formative years and as her first fieldwork experience.[57] She wrote, "Home is also the place to which you come back again and again."[58] And return she did, although not consistently. While she busied herself with her academic career, the town still recognized the adventures of the previous inhabitant. In an article from the September 14, 1928, issue of *The Hammonton News*, a headline reads, "To Study Cannibals: Dr. Margaret Meade [sic], Former Resident Leaves for Work among Natives of South Seas."[59] Decades after her childhood experiences in Hammonton, Margaret still reflected on town traditions with the admiration only possible through nostalgic recollection. On July 16, 1960, Margaret penned a letter to her godson, Daniel Metraux, excitedly writing:

> Just to write July 16th gives me a little thrill because when I was a child, we lived in a town full of Italians and they had a big celebration on July 16, Our Lady of Mount Carmel's Day. They built arbors all along the roads, and a whole amusement park came to town, and there was a band and a parade and firecrackers.[60]

Today, a casual observer would have a difficult time identifying the former Meade property. Martha Meade's six-acre farm, purchased in 1903, was taken by power of attorney from Margaret's grandmother by her father and sold in 1910 after his tryst with another woman. The Meades left, and the property changed hands several times through the years, and fire eventually destroyed the original home.[61] Now, the area is populated with development-tract homes, and the configuration of the old property is all but gone. The only remnants of Margaret's childhood are several declining trees that still stand in the face of urban growth. While the physical house has been lost to the past, the Meades deserve continued remembrance; just as Margaret continued to remember Hammonton throughout her life.

Endnotes

Patricia Chappine is an Adjunct Professor at Stockton University where she teaches courses in Holocaust and Genocide Studies and Women's and Gender Studies. She earned a bachelor's degree in sociology and a master's degree in Holocaust and Genocide Studies from Stockton University and is currently a doctoral student in the History and Culture Program at Drew University. She recently wrote a book titled *New Jersey Women in World War II*, published by the History Press.

Mark Demitroff, an Adjunct Instructor of Geology at Stockton University, grew up on a Pinelands poultry farm. He lectures and publishes widely on land-surface processes, past permafrost, and Pine Barrens geography. Mark practices as a NJ Certified Tree Expert (#285), and serves on the boards of the US Permafrost Association, the South Jersey Culture & History Center, and the Vineland Historical & Antiquarian Society. http://loki.stockton.edu/~demitrom/home.html.

1. Jonathan Berger and John W. Sinton, *Water, Earth, and Fire: Land Use and Environmental Planning in the New Jersey Pine Barrens* (Baltimore, MD: The Johns Hopkins University Press, 1985), 98.
2. H. W. Wilbur and W. B. Hand, *Illustrated History of the Town of Hammonton: With an Account of Its Soil, Climate and Industries* (Hammonton, NJ: The Mirror Steam Printing Co., 1889; 1977 reprint, Hammonton Historical Society), 7.
3. Bill Lockhart, Beau Schreiver, Bill Lindsey, and Carol Serr, "Companies Owned by the Coffin Family," *Encyclopedia of Manufacturer's Marks on Glass Containers: C* (Society for Historical Archaeology), 299, accessed October 3, 2016, https://sha.org/bottle/pdffiles/Coffin.pdf.
4. Hammonton Centennial Committee, *The Story of Hammonton's 100th Anniversary: 1866 – 1966* (Hammonton, NJ: Historical Society of Hammonton, 1966).
5. Elizabeth Marsh, "The Southern Pine Barrens: an Ethnic Archipelago," in *Natural and Cultural Resources of the New Jersey Pine Barrens: Inputs and Research Needs for Planning. Proceedings and Papers of the First Research Conference on the New Jersey Pine Barrens, Atlantic City, N.J., May 22 – 23, 1978,* ed. John W. Sinton (Pomona, NJ: Richard Stockton State College, 1979), 192-98.
6. Mark Demitroff, "Sugar Sand Opportunity: Landscape and People of the Pine Barrens," *Vernacular Architecture Newsletter* (Summer 2014), accessed October 3, 2016, http://vafnewsletter.blogspot.com/2014/07/sugar-sand-opportunity-landscape-and.html.
7. Emily F. Meade, "Italian Immigration into the South," *South Atlantic Quarterly* 4 (June 1905): 217-23.
8. Emily F. Meade, "The Italian on the Land: A Study in Immigration," *Bulletin of the Bureau of Labor* 70 (1907) (reprinted in 1992, Hammonton Historical Society), 1-78.
9. The original spelling "Meade" began to modify, often interchangeably to "Mead" during the Hammonton period (Mark Demitroff, *Bella Vita Major Subdivision. Pinelands Cultural Survey, Pinelands Application #2005-0078.001*, 6. Internal report Buckhorn Garden Service, Inc. submitted to Churchill Consulting Engineers, Berlin, NJ).
10. Nancy C. Lutkehaus, *Margaret Mead: The Making of an American Icon* (Princeton, NJ: Princeton University Press, 2008), 1.
11. Ibid., 5.
12. Ibid., 5–6.
13. Richard F. Ericson, "Society for General Systems Research at Twenty-five: What Agenda for Our Second Quarter Century?" *Behavioral Science* 24, 4 (1979): 225–37.
14. Betty Friedan wrote *The Feminine Mystique*, first published in 1963.
15. Ericson, "Society," 25.
16. Margaret Mead, *Blackberry Winter: My Earlier Years* (New York: William Morrow, 1972), 45.
17. Ibid., 21.
18. Ibid., 12.
19. Emily Fogg Meade, a suffragist, brought young Margaret to rallies (Lutkehaus, *Margaret Mead*, 32). Some Hammontonians speculate that the Meads' association with this women's rights movement irked residents (personal communication, Charles N. "Chic" Mitidieri, April 2, 2016), who viewed suffragists as meddling outsiders. Appeals for better working conditions threatened the prosperity of the town's garment industry, and calls for the prohibition of alcohol were counter to the wine culture brought from Europe. In Hammonton, where sour "wine is a substitute for coffee or tea" every Italian farmer had a small vineyard (see below, Dillingham, *Immigrants in Industries*, 111).
20. Elizabeth G. Messina, "Perversions of Knowledge: Confronting Racist Ideologies behind Intelligence Testing," in *Anti-Italianism: Essays on Prejudice,* eds. William J. Connell and Fred Gardaphe (New York: Palgrave Macmillan, 2010), 54.
21. William Paul Dillingham, *Immigrants in Industries (in Twenty-Five Parts), Part 24: Recent Immigrants in Agriculture* Vol. I, Document No. 633, Reports of the Immigration Commission (Washington, DC: Government Printing Office, 1911), 96.
22. Ibid., 41.
23. Ibid., 43.
24. Ibid.
25. While Italians first arrived in Hammonton in 1868, their full presence was not felt in the local workforce until 1877. See also Dillingham, *Immigrants in Industries,* 100.
26. Dillingham, *Immigrants in Industries*, 42.
27. Ibid., 43.
28. Margaret's caution over intelligence testing passed down to her Barnard College roommate, Louise Rosenblatt, an Atlantic City-born Professor of Literature who became an outspoken critic of the 2001 "No Child Left Behind Act," which heavily relies on one-size-fits-all testing. See J. M. Connell, "Continue to Explore: In Memory of Louise Rosenblatt (1904 – 2005)," *Education & Culture* 21 (2005): 63-79.
29. Mark Demitroff, *Bella Vita Major Subdivision,* 21, 13.
30. Atlantic County Clerk's Office, Deed Book 292, 164, Lydia C. Cauffman to Martha A. Meade, August 19, 1902,

recorded September 3, 1902. Demitroff, *Bella Vita*, 6.
31 Lutkehaus, *Margaret Mead*, 28.
32 Emily Fogg Meade, *The Italian on the Land*, 1.
33 Ibid., 2.
34 Ibid.
35 Ibid.
36 Ibid., 4.
37 Ibid., 5.
38 Ibid.
39 Dillingham, *Immigrants in Industries*, 95-96.
40 Ibid., 54.
41 Ibid., 10.
42 Ibid.
43 The Hammonton property with home, in actuality approximately six acres, was located on Fairview Avenue. Demitroff, *Bella Vita Major Subdivision*, 10.
44 The influence of Margaret's father has likely been underappreciated. McLean and Jones indicate Edward was a major figure in his own right who taught by the application of practical case methodology (as did the anthropologist), and his love of facts mirrored Margaret's academic approach. Paula A. McLean and D. G. Brian Jones, "Edward Sherwood Mead (1874 – 1956): A Pioneer in Finance Education," *European Business Review* 19, 2 (2007): 118.
45 Ibid., 120.
46 Edward Sherwood Mead, *Trust Finance: A Study of the Genesis, Organization, and Management of Industrial Combinations* (New York: D. Appleton and Co, 1903), 47.
47 Edward Sherwood Mead, "The Work of the Promoter," in *The Making of America: Industry & Finance* Vol. III, ed. Robert M. LaFollette (Philadelphia: J. D. Morris and Co., 1905), 243.
48 McLean and Jones, "Edward Sherwood Mead," 243.
49 Jane Howard, *Margaret Mead: A Life* (New York: Ballantine Books, 1984), 28.
50 Ibid., 27.
51 Lois Banner, *Intertwined Lives: Margaret Mead, Ruth Benedict, and Their Circle* (New York, Alfred A. Knopf, 2003), 18.
52 Mead, *Blackberry Winter*, 35.
53 Lenora Foerstel and Angela Gilliam, eds. *Confronting the Margaret Mead Legacy: Scholarship, Empire, and the South Pacific* (Philadelphia: Temple University Press, 1992), 107-108.
54 Ibid.
55 Ibid., 97.
56 Barbara Kirshenblatt-Gimblett, Introduction, *Life is with People: The Culture of the Shtetl*, by Mark Zborowski and Elizabeth Herzog (New York: Schocken, 1995), 12-13.
57 Margaret wrote poetry: *Song of Five Springs*, written c. 1927, is a typescript of her verse preserved in the Manuscript Division of the Library of Congress. She prefaced her autobiography with a poem "Blackberry Winter" (Mead, *Blackberry Winter: My Earlier Years*, 1972). The poem and book title memorialize fruit raised at the six-acre lot. Blackberries were then by far the most important commodity in town. An 1896 root-disease epidemic all but wiped out cane blackberry (Dillingham, *Immigrants in Industries*, 110), so farmers switched to vine dewberry. The Black Diamond, a chance dewberry seedling of "Oregon Evergreen," quickly became Hammonton's standard; see George H. Leipe, "The Black Diamond Blackberry" (promotional brochure for G. H. Liepe, Cologne, NJ, c. 1908), 1. Oregon Giant coincidentally originated in the South Sea Islands via Australia; see U. P. Hedrick et al., *The Small Fruits of New York. Annnual Report . . .* (1925): 189. Mead worked in Samoa and Papua New Guinea. Dewberry is present in the latter place (see J. L. C. H. van Valkenburg, "Rubus L." *Plant Resources of South-East Asia* 12.2 [2001]: 477-80), but not the former place (see J. C. Space and T. Flynn, "Observations on Invasive Plant Species in American Samoa," *Pacific Island Ecosystems at Risk* [2000], accessed October 3, 2016, http://www.hear.org/pier/reports/asreport.htm).
58 Mead, *Blackberry Winter*, 13.
59 Lutkehaus, *Margaret Mead*, 112.
60 Margaret Caffrey and Patricia Francis, eds. *To Cherish the Life of the World: The Selected Letters of Margaret Mead* (New York: Basic Books, 2006), 364.
61 Demitroff, *Bella Vita Major Subdivision*, 10.

Joe's Diner Matchbook. In 1892 a Philadelphia lawyer patented the first matchbook. Two years later the Diamond Match Company purchased the rights to the design, and matchbooks became instant miniature billboards as the preponderance of Americans enjoyed tobacco products. Joe's Diner, pictured here, was located at 6th Terrace and the White House Pike in Egg Harbor City, New Jersey. The Ideal Diner replaced this old dining car around 1940 and now the Harbor Diner occupies the same site.

World War I and the Pine Barrens.
From a commonly held viewpoint of virtual worthlessness, sections of the Pine Barrens drew the interest of the military-industrial complex as the United States entered the First World War. This "worthless" land offered ideal potential sites for training bases, shell-loading plants, and ordnance proving grounds. Thousands of sylvan acres and habitats suddenly yielded to the will of government and private enterprise. The construction of Camp Dix, a major basic training facility, Camp Kendrick, for chemical warfare training, along with shell-loading plants like Amatol and Belcoville, brought profound change to parts of the Pine Barrens during 1917 – 1918. For Camp Dix, the federal government acquired 8,000 acres. Camp Kendrick, in Ocean County, was established on a

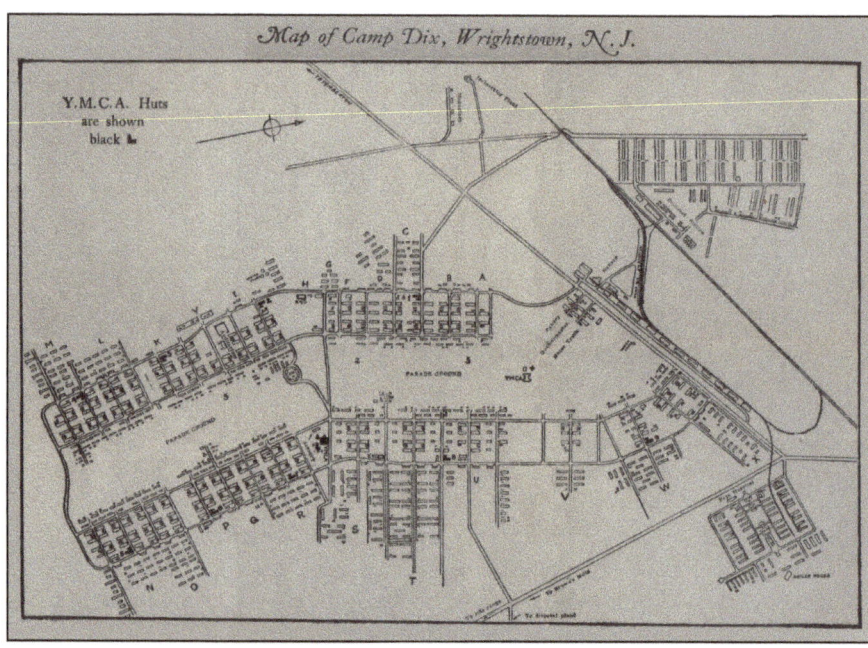

private munitions proving grounds constructed for the Russian Czar and covered 754 acres. Built and operated by the Atlantic Loading Company, the production and residential facility at Amatol consumed 6,000 acres. The Bethlehem Loading Company established Belcoville on 5,000 acres. All of these military training and ordnance facilities were built and made operational in record time. While Camp Dix, renamed Fort Dix in 1939, remains an active military base and Camp Kendrick formed the nucleus of the Lakehurst Naval Air Station, Amatol and Belcoville were shuttered soon after hostilities ceased in Europe and the belligerents signed the armistice. When the plants completed their contract work, the federal government ordered the Amatol and Belcoville factories and towns dismantled and sold, along with the acquired land, at auction. The Atlantic County Game Preserve acquired a large parcel of land associated with Belcoville and used it as a private hunting club. Some of the Belcoville buildings still stand, including the school. A portion of Amatol became the Atlantic City Speedway, a wooden racetrack for early automobile races. Today, only the Amatol administration building survives, which had served as a state police barracks before building a new barracks. For those who know where to look, large concrete remnants can still be found in the woods where Amatol and Belcoville once operated. Nature, however, is slowly reclaiming and removing the scars left behind by the effects of a war prosecuted one hundred years ago, far away across the Atlantic Ocean in Europe.

A Day on the Bay with Waterman Phil Andersen

Susan Allen

A waterman's wardrobe—waders, muck boots and gloves—neatly hang on a clothesline and wall rack soaking up the warm, morning sun pouring into Phil Andersen's Oyster Creek crab house, in Leeds Point, New Jersey. Below, friends watch from the dock as Phil and his crabbing partner, Bobby Dianjoell, head out into the bay in their floating office.

From the Greek language, *Callinectes sapidus* (Atlantic blue crab) translates to beautiful swimmer. Flaunting their vibrant blue and red-orange pinchers, these crustaceans gracefully speed through aquatic forests of eelgrass.

Phil steers to a buoy and hauls a crab pot out of the water. Bobby then takes over emptying the catch into a tub quickly measuring and sorting crabs into one of three bushel-sized baskets based on size and gender. Pots are restocked with bunker and returned to the bay. The Beatles and other classic tunes play on satellite radio as this process is repeated down the bay.

A Day on the Bay

Bobby measures the catch and secures a lid onto a full basket of live crabs, ready for market.

(Below) A bald eagle is just one of the many species of birds that Phil and Bobby see on the marsh. Ospreys are seen on nesting platforms where they raise their young, and gulls often follow the boat for bait scraps.

Phil, who served his country as a marine, is just over 70 years old, but four decades of life on the bay have kept him young. He still wakes up each morning excited to go to work.

A Day on the Bay

The crab house is like a second home. From April through November, Phil is crabbing, and during the months he's not working on the water, he's hunting waterfowl and watching wildlife.

Wharf, Newport, Cumberland County, New Jersey. In 1909 – 1910, a Philadelphia steamboat dealer named Ulysses Grant Bethel purchased a fumigating steamer named the Louis Pasteur. She was built and launched during 1889 in Wilmington, Delaware, for the United States Marine-Hospital Service and assigned to the USMHS station at Reedy Point, Port Penn, Delaware. When constructed, the iron-hulled steamer cost the federal government $22,500. Dimensions of the steamer were: 78' 8" long; 16' 6" breadth; 6' 3" draft; 62 gross tonnage and 42 net tonnage. Bethel decided not to sell the steamer and, after some rehabilitation work, renamed the steamer the Helen Bethel for his six-year-old daughter, Helen V. Bethel. He put the boat to work with a crew of three as both a tugboat and a freight boat using Philadelphia, Pennsylvania, as the steamer's homeport. The steamer was a regular traveler on the Maurice River and other Down Jersey watercourses. It appears her last year of service was 1919, when Bethel probably scrapped the boat. In this view, taken circa 1915, the Helen Bethel has carefully picked her way up the meandering Nantuxent Creek, turned, and then tied up at Newport or East Landing in Downe Township, Cumberland County, New Jersey. While the 1905 United States Coast Pilot does not even mention Nantuxent Creek, the 1916 edition of the same work reports, Nantuxent Creek, 6¼ miles east-southeastward of Ship John Shoal lighthouse, has a depth of about 5 feet in the entrance, and is navigable at high water to within about one mile of the village of Newport. It is used only by local oyster boats (p. 84). You can see five or six of those oyster boats in the background with their masts reaching for the heavens out along the marshes that stretch to the horizon on the way out to the Delaware River. Farmers are driving their wagons up to boat to unload truck baskets filled with tomatoes bound for Campbell Soup in Camden or, perhaps, the P. J. Ritter Company in Bridgeton for ketchup production. Note the loaded baskets stacked in the stern of the vessel and also the "flying bridge" on the boat, where the master has a firm grip on the wheel with no protective cabin surrounding him.

South Jersey Fruit Picking Tickets

Richard Watson

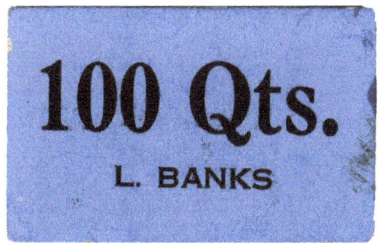
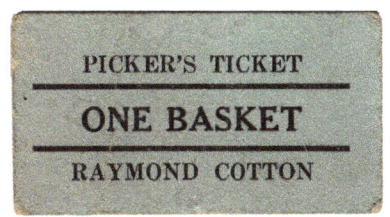

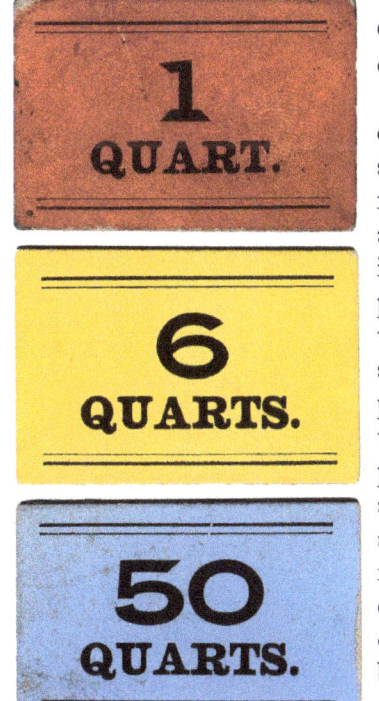

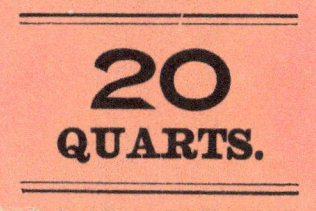
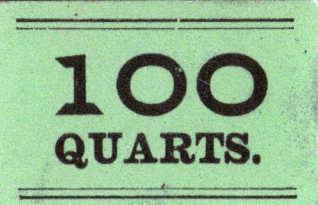

In the early days, farmers were limited to selling their produce within the distance that horse drawn wagons could travel before the delicate cargo spoiled. With the arrival of the railroads during the second half of the nineteenth century, farmers discovered a greatly expanded market for their crops.[1] Commission merchants established themselves in the big cities and helped the rural growers find buyers for their produce. Following the Civil War, improvements in refrigeration further extended markets for local produce. Perishable fruits could now be carried farther to reach important shipping hubs in major mid-Western, Southern, and New England cities. In many places, the iron rails opened up once isolated or distant areas to cultivation. Indeed, more than a few important farming districts owe their very existence to the arrival of the railroad.

These factors and others contributed to a shift from subsistence farming to commercial agriculture, particularly in the prosperous postbellum years of the 1860s. Farmers soon enlarged their plantations, enabling them to specialize in particular crops, being assured that their fruits and vegetables could be readily sold. With this evolution came great opportunity for farmers, but it presented new challenges as well. In particular, picking large crops of berries, orchard fruits, and vegetables proved extremely labor intensive. No longer could family, friends, neighbors and a few hired day laborers harvest the crops. Growers quickly found that their greater acreage required many more workers at harvest time. Outsiders, usually from neighboring cities and frequently from the latest immigrant class, arrived when the crops were ready to be picked. Developing effective methods for managing these itinerant workers, while maintaining accurate accounts, urgently required resolution.

Farmers quickly learned that they could better motivate their new seasonal workers with pay based on the quantity of produce harvested. The pickers would travel out to the fields with harvest baskets or bushel boxes; when full, the laborer would carry them to a checking station, where a foreman or clerk would credit each worker in a notebook or journal. Each picker could then have their quarts, bushels or other measures tallied on payday and settlement could be made.

The workers kept track of their own labors, but the burden of maintaining proper records for each picker fell squarely on the grower's shoulders. If a disagreement arose on payday, many plantation owners were obliged to accept their workers account.[2] Over time, farmers sought a more precise system for tracking a worker's productivity and proper remuneration. Some began using metal tokens or checks to track the harvested

Strawberry pickers in the field at William Parry's plantation in Cinnaminson, New Jersey. Parry also operated the Pomona Nursery in that area. Indeed, a section of Cinnaminson is still known by the name of Parry. From *Harper's Weekly*, July 3, 1869.

produce each picker brought to the checking station. This proved to be a more exacting and foolproof system than attempting to record each picker's crop harvests. The tokens usually featured a farmer's name or initials stamped on them; they could be exchanged at the end of

Early brass and tin picker tokens from the George W. Russ farm in Delanco, New Jersey.

the season or even the end of the day or week, depending on the terms, for hard currency. With this new payment arrangement, farmers no longer needed an abundance of cash on hand. This method virtually eliminated arguments over the credibility of the accounts on both the farmers' and the workers' ends and made the laborer responsible for maintaining his or her own collection of tokens.

The tokens were often made from brass, aluminum, tin or iron. They might have first been used for strawberry picking in Anne Arundel County, Maryland, dating back to as early as the 1850s.[3] The tokens were also stamped to identify different denominations, allowing smaller values to be exchanged for larger ones. When pickers collected enough one-basket tokens, they could be swapped for five, twenty-five, or even one-hundred-basket tokens. In some areas, these metal checks endured for many years. Packinghouses and canneries used the same system for payment as well, as the metal tokens proved to be quite durable in these manually intensive settings.

In 1871, Andrew A. Baker of Camden, New Jersey, patented a holder for metallic fruit picker checks. This newly designed field box, or cash register, utilized vertical metal fingers to organize various checks that featured a hole drilled in the center. The tokens could be slid onto

Picking Tickets

or removed from the upright rods as needed. In Baker's Fruit-Growers' Check-Holder, each denomination had a different shape, allowing for easier identification. Even though evidence of this type of organizer exists, their use is relatively unknown, as many farmers were likely searching for a more economic alternative.

An example of Andrew Baker's fruit pickers' check holder: a field box or cash register that was used to organize the metallic picker checks.

Many growers began to use pasteboard tokens, or tickets, that could be printed in great quantities at a low cost. Using tickets soon became the primary method of managing the accounts of berry pickers and other types of farm laborers. The produce would be carried to a packinghouse or checking station on the edge of the field, where workers would exchange the filled containers for the cardboard checks. With this system, the workers accumulated a cache of tickets, often trading lower valued checks for tickets of higher value. The various tickets were usually printed on different color stock to more easily identify different values.[4] On payday, the workers returned the tickets to the grower and exchanged them for proper compensation.

The following newspaper article from 1896 describes the payment system for berry pickers in Hammonton:

During the berry season there are about 3000 Italians in Hammonton and vicinity, a number considerably over the native population of the place. To keep these people within bounds, and prevent them from deserting the berry fields for South Eighth Street, as they are sometimes inclined to do when they cannot make as much money as they desire, no money is paid out to them under any circumstances, except, perhaps, a trifle now and then on account. In lieu of cash they are given tickets, which represent the number of quarts of berries they pick. When the season is over these tickets are cashed either by the owner of the berry patch or at the stores in Hammonton, where these tickets pass as money for the purchase of goods, but are not convertible into cash.[5]

Some farmers paid their pickers more frequently; often at the end of the week.[6] This practice likely became more common, as securing labor during the busy harvest season grew increasingly difficult. Eventually, growers bused the pickers from the city to the farm daily, and on some of these farms, settlement with the pickers was made at the end of each day.

Picker tickets were frequently secured in a "field box" like this one. Some boxes were metal and others made from wood. Often these ticket organizers were hand-crafted or fashioned from other repurposed boxes.

As mentioned, these small cardstock tickets quickly morphed into a form of currency on the farms. They even served as a commonplace currency in neighboring towns. Many of the merchants in the berry-picking districts accepted tickets as payment for goods and services,

53

From "Success with Small Fruits."

knowing they could readily be exchanged with the local farmers for cash.[7] Indeed, most storekeepers welcomed the extra business during the busy harvest season. There were benefits for the grower as well. Storekeepers would accumulate tickets in lots and redeem them with the farmer for a bank check. Farmers thus avoided the necessity of keeping large amounts of cash on hand.[8] In some areas, vendors would visit the fields to sell pies, gingerbread and other "nondescript edibles."[9] Pickers could exchange their tickets for such provisions, and the peddlers would then take the checks to the farmer for redemption. Surprisingly, a similar practice still continues to this day in a few places. Now, however, the hawkers arrive in food trucks to the farms. Reportedly, tickets are still used as a form of currency on a few plantations.

In some agricultural areas, the use of picker checks or tickets dominated harvests and the practice lasted for many years. Strawberry tickets were used extensively along the Chesapeake's Eastern Shore or Delmarva Peninsula where hundreds of farms shipped trainloads of the ripened fruit to cities near and far. The Ozarks region in Missouri and Oklahoma formed another large strawberry center where the use of picker tickets was common. Dewberry tickets were prevalent in certain areas, most notably in parts of North Carolina. Countless other regions specialized in growing these berries and other varieties of small fruit. Due to the demand for more workers during harvest season, the use of picking tickets expanded throughout much of the country.

South Jersey

In no small way, New Jersey owes its nickname "The Garden State" to the bountiful farms in its lower counties. At one time, strawberries grown in South Jersey were the first to reach market. Farmers grew raspberries and blackberries extensively in some areas. Apple and peach orchards produced major crops in the Garden State as well. Other important varieties of produce grown in New Jersey are asparagus, bell peppers, eggplant, endives, lettuce and spinach. Cabbages, snap peas, and of course corn and tomatoes are also raised in this state.

A thriving cranberry industry developed in New Jersey shortly after commercial production first began on Cape Cod. The blueberry, another important fruit, first underwent cultivatation in New Jersey. Elizabeth White and Frederick Coville developed improved varieties of this native fruit on the edge of the Jersey Pines near Pemberton. Both the cranberry and the blueberry are counted among the Garden State's most valuable agricultural products.

Vendors selling their "nondescript edibles" to strawberry pickers in the field. From "Success with Small Fruits."

Picker tickets from the Van Sciver farm that was once active in Willingboro, New Jersey.

Picking Tickets

A young woman picking cranberries into a one-peck box on a bog in Burlington County. *Photograph by Arthur Rothstein, Library of Congress collection.*

Cranberry Culture

The extensive cultivation of the cranberry began in New Jersey during the late 1860s. Each fall thereafter witnessed thousands of pickers arriving, often Italian immigrants from Philadelphia. Whole trainloads of these workers traveled to Medford, Pemberton, Hammonton, and other rail stops near the cranberry districts. From there, wagons—and, in later days, trucks—shuttled the pickers to the remote bogs in the Pines. Once there, the workers began the arduous task of bringing in the crop.

Unlike today's modern harvest methods, cranberries once required hand-picking. Originally, the laborers were expected to pick into baskets, which they then carried to the edge of the bog and dumped into bags. At day's end, wagons transported the bags to the packinghouse, where the boss tallied the contents. This additional handling proved injurious to the fruit, and the process resulted in idle time for weary workers after long hours of picking. For these counterproductive reasons, and to avoid any disagreement over accounts, New Jersey grower J. J. White advocated the use of tickets in the cranberry bogs.[10] White voiced his opinion in a book he wrote on cranberry culture, published in 1870.

Cranberry growers soon began sending their workers into the bogs with one-peck boxes. These usually featured pine slab construction and metal handles. This arrangement allowed pickers to carry two containers in each hand as they carried the berries from the bog. Barrels and, later, one-bushel crates called "Jersey long boxes," stood stacked on the edge of the bogs. The pickers would carry their collected fruit to these convenient checking stations, where the so-called "bushel man" would exchange the berries for cardboard tickets, which each picker would safeguard until they could be exchanged for cash on payday.

Similar to those used for other varietal fruits, cranberry tickets featured various values printed on their face. Assorted cardstock colors provided ease in counting. Pickers frequently traded these tickets for higher denominations, making holding the tickets more convenient. Thus four "1 Peck" tickets could be exchanged with the foreman for a "1 Bushel" ticket; even the "1 Bushel" tickets could be exchanged for ones of larger value.

This woman is receiving a picker ticket from the bushel man after delivering her one-peck boxes of cranberries. *Photograph by Arthur Rothstein, Library of Congress collection.*

Owing to the remoteness of many New Jersey bogs, the pickers and their families were generally housed in barracks-like buildings where they remained throughout the harvest season. As with many other farms, the accounts of the pickers on the bogs were usually settled at the end of the harvest. Occasionally the farm owners would extend some credit to their workers for the purchase of necessities. In fact, many of the larger cranberry growers had general stores that would accept the tickets as payment for their goods.

Journal entry from Sorden's cranberry meadow at Goshen shows Abraham Sorden receiving $1.25 per day for handing out tickets to the pickers in 1893. William P. Sorden Cranberry Logbook for 1893–1894. *Courtesy of the Richard Watson collection.*

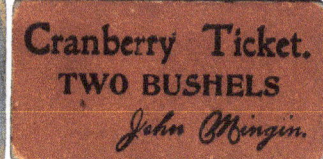

Two early cranberry tickets from Shamong Township that were used on bogs near Dellet. A pioneer named Wiliam R. Braddock began growing the fruit there before 1850. Braddock and his sons are supposed to be the first Jerseymen to plant improved varieties by purchasing cranberry vines from Cape Cod.

Often the utter isolation of the bogs afforded no alternative to the company shop and put workers at the mercy of the store keepers who could charge a premium for the merchandise they stocked.

Budd's Bogs

Theodore Budd of Pemberton was among the first in New Jersey to begin growing cranberries. Born at Buddtown in Southampton, he built his first bogs in 1859 near Sheep Pen Hill, located between Buddtown and Ong's Hat. Budd was instrumental in organizing the first ever cranberry growers association when in 1864 he placed an advertisement in local newspapers inviting interested parties to meet him at Colkitt's Hotel in Vincentown to discuss the incipient industry.

This pioneer cranberry grower proved quite successful in his endeavor. Soon sons, Clifford and Isaac, united with their father in this pursuit and operated under the name Theodore Budd and Sons. The Budds expanded the bogs at Sheep Pen Hill along with planting many more acres of vines at a place known as Retreat, situated just a short distance from Buddtown.

Clifford Budd took charge of the family's cranberry empire after the death of his father and eventually acquired his brother Isaac's interest in the enterprise. Joining this second-generation grower was his son, Theodore H. Budd, who entered the cranberry business in 1909. All of these men remained active in the various cranberry associations that followed the one their forbear started.

When the cultivated blueberry was first developed in New Jersey, the Budd family was among the earliest to embrace this emergent industry. They planted at least 60 acres of the fruit at Retreat and owned a larger berry production farm in North Carolina.[11]

Evans & Wills

Two Quakers named Joseph Evans and Joshua Wills were also among the first in New Jersey to commence cultivating cranberries. Evans owned the Hillside Farm near Marlton and Wills was a farmer at Stokelan in Medford. Joseph Evans had married Joshua's sister Lydia Wills in 1868 and the brothers-in-law soon became good friends. Shortly thereafter, the two partnered in purchasing a tract of land called Friendship Neck in Washington Township, Burlington County.[12] There they eventually succeeded in establishing an extensive cranberry plantation in the heart of the Pines and a small village named Friendship developed around a sizable packing house that the partners erected to process the fruit. For decades, Evans and Wills continued to purchase adjoining acreage and expanded their bogs as

the opportunities arose. The settlement at Friendship was sometimes referred to as Quaker and even had its own one-room schoolhouse.

The two partners also bought land in Medford Township along the road to Manahawkin (today known simply as Hawkin Road) and called the bogs they built there Quoexin. Evans and Wills expanded this property when they subsequently purchased the farm of Benjamin Mingin. They later added the cranberry bogs of Edmund Braddock and those of Israel Garwood to the property. Quoexin is one of just two cranberry operations that remain active in Medford Township.

About 1903 Evans and Wills purchased the Willow Farm property between Taunton and Marlton. As its name suggests, the farm originally grew willow trees for basket making, but a man named Gillingham later established cranberry bogs there. The Evans family grew cranberries on that property until the early 1970s when they sold it for the construction of the King's Grant development.

Joseph Evans died in 1909, but the enormous cranberry enterprise continued under the management of Joshua Wills for the benefit of the Evans estate. In 1931 the parties incorporated under the name of Evans & Wills[13] and remained an active concern until the 1950s, when the two families made a division of the properties. Around that time, Joseph Evans' heirs purchased a cranberry bog property near the Willow Farm and operated that string of bogs separate from the partnership with Wills. These bogs, located along Black Run at a place called Cold Spring were also known as the Shanty Bogs. Nearby, it appears the Joseph Evans Estate also operated the Shafer Bogs and Buzby's Bogs in a similar manner.

Joseph Wharton

Beginning in 1876 with his purchase of Batsto, Joseph Wharton started acquiring huge parcels of land in the New Jersey Pine Barrens with the idea of exporting the pure water from the area's vast aquifers to Philadelphia. After the New Jersey Governor threatened to stop Wharton and the Philadelphia City Council lost interest in his scheme, the Pennsylvania industrialist turned to farming and other pursuits. Wharton found many parts of his vast landholdings conducive for cultivating cranberries and into this endeavor he directed much effort. He improved existing cranberry bogs on his property and, in a few cases, laid out new meadows.

Wharton grew the tart fruit near Batsto, Atsion, Ancora, and even in the vicinity of the old paper mill at Harrisville. He converted the former cotton mill at Atsion into a packing house and shipped carloads of cranberries via trains from that station.

Before his death in 1909, Wharton had planned to build between 500 and 1000 acres of cranberry bogs in

Camden, Burlington, and Atlantic Counties.[14] Part of his expansion policy included planting vines along a branch of the Tulpehocken stream call the Featherbed Branch. This plan was carried out for Wharton's estate with the first fifty acres of vines being set out in 1909. These bogs, built adjacent to the Friendship bogs of Evans and Wills, subsequently underwent expansion and became known as the Sandy Ridge Bogs.

Blueberries

A hundred years ago, residents of the Jersey Pine Barrens would venture into the woods each spring and gather the wild blueberries and huckleberries that grew prolifically in some areas. Many had their favorite patches that they returned to year after year, drawn there by the pervasiveness of these flavorful berries.

About 1910, Elizabeth Coleman White, daughter of famed cranberry grower Joseph J. White, became interested in the idea of developing commercially successful varieties of these wild blueberries at Whitesbog, near Browns Mills in Pemberton Township, Burlington County. She and her father contacted a botanist from the U.S. Department of Agriculture named Dr. Fredrick V. Coville who had written about early attempts at propagating the blueberry bush. Coville accepted an invitation to Whitesbog where he and Elizabeth White began hybridizing the wild plants that were native to the Jersey Pines.

As the story goes, Coville and White enlisted the help of local residents to find promising plants with large fruit and a pleasing taste. The Pineys who went searching in the woods received two dollars for a desirable specimen and the varieties then propagated from these bushes were sometimes named in their honor.

By 1916 the first ever commercial crop of cultivated blueberries was harvested at Whitesbog and since that time New Jersey has boasted a thriving blueberry industry. Thousands of workers have flocked to the Pines to harvest blueberries each summer and to bring in the cranberry crop each fall. Like other fruit farmers, many blueberry growers adopted the method of issuing berry tickets to their workers during the picking season.

The general store at Whitesbog was surely a busy place during the cranberry and blueberry harvest. Picker tickets would have been readily accepted for the purchase of merchandise.

Though places like Pemberton and Hammonton became major blueberry districts, hundreds of farmers began growing the popular fruit all throughout the pine belt.

CUTTS BROTHERS

In 1929, four brothers from Tabernacle, Burlington County, bought some land in Bass River Township and began building cranberry bogs. The Cutts brothers knew something of the business as their father had begun growing cranberries about the year 1900 near a place called Goose Pond, not far from the family's home. The boys experienced great success in their endeavor and quickly added thousands of acres to their original purchase. One of their acquisitions included the long established Calico meadow, first planted in 1866.

The Cutts entered the blueberry business in 1933 and soon the brothers had 100 acres of bushes planted on their property.[15] For a long time the four siblings were counted among the largest blueberry growers in the world and even bought 1500 acres near Ivanhoe, North Carolina, on which to cultivate the berries. Alongside their fields in Bass River, they erected a substantial packing house for the fruit and an extensive labor camp to house the pickers during the busy harvest season.

Upper – Blueberry tickets used by Shirley Thompson at Retreat near Vincentown, New Jersey.

Middle – Picker tickets of Amelia and Richard Green who grew blueberries near Chatsworth.

Lower – Wills and Kahoun were also berry farmers with plantings near Chatsworth.

Picking Tickets

Order Berry Tickets Now

Printing Tickets

Most rural towns did not possess their own printing shops. Occasionally farmers would travel to metropolitan centers to have their tickets printed; however, growers found that many of the local newspapers also had a small print shop that would accommodate their berry ticket needs. In Medford, the *Central Record* catered to the local growers of cranberries, blueberries, strawberries as well as other fruits or vegetables. A journal of "job work" for the years 1931 to 1941 shows that scores of farmers used this shop to print their tickets. Berry growers and other farmers from Medford, Southampton, Tabernacle and Shamong are listed all throughout the work journal.

Other newspapers handled the printing needs of local growers too. *The Burlington County Times Advertiser* serviced farmers in the Pemberton area. The *New Jersey Courier* from Toms River and the *Red Bank Register* also advertised ticket printing for farmers in those parts of New Jersey.[16] In Hammonton a paper called the *South-Jersey Republican* offered to print berry tickets for local growers as early as 1880. Such advertisements appeared regularly in that publication for decades. The *Bridgeton Evening News* and the *Woodbury Daily Times* printed picker tickets for farmers as well.

The selection of tickets below are typical of those used in the Hammonton area for many years. These checks were most certainly printed by the *South-Jersey Republican* office.

Order Berry Tickets Now,— The best you ever saw, and Worth fully twice the price } Printed by HOYT & SON Next to Post Office

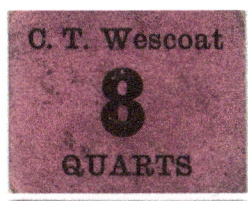
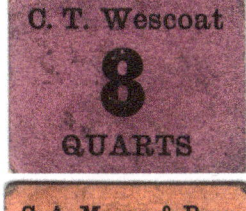

☞ BERRY TICKETS !!
We would inform any fruit growers who may be in need of berry tickets, that we are fully prepared to give them *just what they want* and at the lowest prices. Give us a call and go away satisfied.

☞ Have you a full supply and good assortment of berry picker tickets? If not, you can have them printed for a fair price, at the REPUBLICAN office.

☞ Everybody is pleased with our berry picker tickets. They prevent cheating, save time, enable every picker to keep an account of his work, don't cost much, and last for years. We have printed many thousands of them, yet can print as many more. Bring in your orders.

Advertisements from the *South-Jersey Republican* —June 5, 1880; May 26, 1888; June 16, 1888.

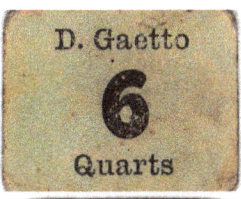
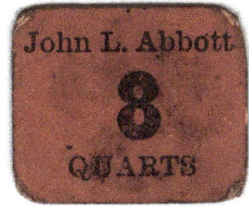

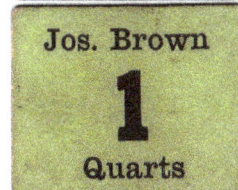

Tickets with printed, stamped, or hand-written numbers helped farmers maintain accurate harvest records.

While the use of picker tickets had some significant advantages over other methods, the system was not perfect. Sometimes the picker misplaced the small tickets and presumably reports of thefts proved common. Farmers also encountered difficulty in tracking the daily picking measures in comparison to the number of tickets issued. For this reason, some farmers began using tickets printed with consecutive numbers. This practice not only made a check unique but also allowed the farmer to easily tabulate each day's work. The grower would simply note the number of the first and last ticket issued each day and subtract to determine the quantity of fruit picked. The method told the farmer exactly what each day's picking costs should be and also provided a perfect check on the person handing out the tickets. The farmer knew that slight discrepancies between picked fruit and issued tickets would occur from time to time and could be chalked up to honest mistakes, but large differences could be addressed immediately.[17]

Some farmers found it useful to use consecutively numbered movie theater-style tickets that came in rolls of 2000 and could be affordably printed with a grower's name. This style of check was thin, rather delicate, and probably intended for one-time use, though some frugal farmers seem to have re-issued them from year to year. The Globe Ticket Company, in center-city Philadelphia, printed most of the "roll" tickets used in South Jersey. Globe even advertised in the national trade publication, *Cranberries*.

Sometime before 1900, a newer system was developed that many growers preferred.[18] In this method, pickers received a card or tag printed with rows of numbers. Often the numbers represented common units of measure. When the pickers carried their filled containers to the packing house or checking station, the clerk would register the amount of fruit picked by punching out the appropriate numbers on the card. This method eliminated the handfuls of small tickets that easily suffered damage or loss.[19] The card tickets also prevented theft, since each carried the picker's name.[20] The clerk punched each card with a railroad conductor's punch, usually featuring a specially shaped die[21] that could not be easily duplicated, thereby reducing fraud. The farmer's most trusted foreman guarded the punches and, on many farms, only family members could handle and control the punch.

Many New Jersey blueberry farmers embraced this style of picker ticket card. The two at left were used on farms near New Lisbon, Burlington County. The tag at right was used by New Jersey growers who had blueberry fields in North Carolina. More than a few blueberry farmers from New Jersey had extensive plantations in North Carolina as the fruit ripened several weeks before the Jersey crop came in.

Tales persist from the earlier days when crafty pickers defrauded farmers using razor blades to deftly duplicate the special punch marks on the tickets. Perhaps to counter this, some farmers used two tags for each worker. The picker received one ticket and the clerk retained the other. When the picker delivered the fruit, the clerk placed both tickets together and punched them simultaneously.[22] This system also provided some relief to the picker who may have lost his tag.

To be sure, these old tickets and tags recall an earlier time when farming was the dominant activity in many parts of South Jersey. Over the years, our shrinking farm acreage and a shift toward mechanized picking has significantly reduced the labor force needed at harvest time.

A strip of cranberry tickets used by William Reeves on his cranberry bogs along the McDonalds Branch in Woodland Township. The bogs are surrounded today by the Brendan Byrne State Forest.

Picking Tickets

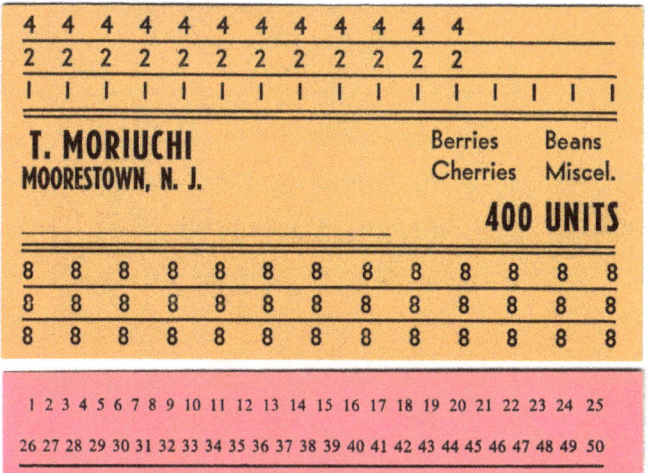

Examples of "punch" cards or picker tags used in South Jersey. The Bertonazzi Bros. farm continues to operate in Vineland.

At the same time, laws governing minimum wage have curtailed the "piece work" pay system that made use of tickets to keep track of each picker's production. Many of our farms have long disappeared, yet these small cardboard artifacts remain a tangible piece of our area's rich agricultural heritage.

Endnotes

Rich Watson grew up in the Taunton Lake section of Medford Township, Burlington County, where he developed a deep appreciation for the area's rich history. A graduate of Rutgers University, Rich has worked in the Lenape Regional High School District for the past 27 years, currently teaching Physics and Principles of Engineering at Seneca High School in Tabernacle. He has spent countless hours exploring the Pine Barrens and researching the region's former industries, its agriculture, and its long forgotten places. Rich is a member of the West Jersey History Roundtable. He and his family make their home in Tabernacle.

Together with his late father, Rich has spent many years gathering picking tickets and tokens from across the country. Readers are encouraged to discuss any of these items with the author by contacting him at: watson.southjerseyhistory@yahoo.com.

1. Henry C. Wallace, "The Farmers and the Railroads," *Proceedings of the Academy of Political Science in the City of New York* 10, 1 (1922): 63-65.
2. Joseph J. White, "Cranberry Culture" (New York: Orange Judd & Co., 1870), 88.
3. Robert D. Leonard Jr., "American Fruit Picker Tokens from Coast to Coast," transcript of address to the Chicago Coin Club, July 11, 2001, http://www.chicagocoinclub.org/chatter/2001/Aug/.
4. "Picking the Berry Crop," *American Gardening* 18, 126 (May 1897): 375-78.
5. "Strawberries in New Jersey. The Mammoth Berry Patches at Hammonton," *Worcester Daily Spy* (Worcester, MA), June 8, 1896, 7.
6. "Picking the Berry Crop," *American Gardening*, 375-78.
7. James Pennewill, "J. Baker Bryan, d. b. a., vs. J. Frederick Brown, p. b. r." *Pennewill's Delaware Reports, Containing Cases Decided in Supreme Court, Superior Court, and Court of General Sessions of the State of Delaware*, Vol. 3 (Wilmington, DE: Law Book Publishers, 1903), 504-508.
8. Wm. E. Schimpf, "Keeping Production Records by Growers of Small Fruit," *Better Fruit, Better Fruit Publishing Company* 15, 1 (July 1920): 4.
9. Edward P. Roe, "Success with Small Fruits" (New York: Dodd, Mead & Company, 1880), 125.
10. Joseph J. White, "Cranberry Culture" (New York: Orange Judd & Co., 1870), 88.
11. Clarence J. Hall, "The Budds of New Jersey: Real Cranberry Growers," *Cranberries, The National Cranberry Magazine* 10, 9 (January 1946): 6-10.
12. Ezra Evans, "A Short Chronicle of Evans & Wills, Inc.," *Minutes of Annual Meeting of Evans & Wills, Inc.*, 1953.
13. Clarence J. Hall, "Sharpless Grandson of Jersey Pioneer," *Cranberries, The National Cranberry Magazine* 10, 10 (February, 1946): 19-20. Business records of Evans & Wills, Inc., are housed in Special Collections & Archives, the Bjork Library, Stockton University.
14. "Putting More Money in Jersey Cranberry," *The Philadelphia Inquirer*, May 24, 1909, 3.
15. Clarence J. Hall, "Cutts Brothers of New Jersey: Sound Operators," *Cranberries, The National Cranberry Magazine* 18, 9 (January 1954): 9-11.
16. *Red Bank Register* (Red Bank, NJ), June 15, 1898, 4.
17. Wm. E. Schimpf, "Keeping Production Records by Growers of Small Fruit," 4.
18. "Picking the Berry Crop," *American Gardening*, 375-78.
19. Arthur D. Dorr, "Berry Picker's Card," *The Rural New Yorker* 71, 4140 (March 2, 1912): 297.
20. "Picking the Berry Crop," *American Gardening*, 375-78.
21. Ibid.
22. Fred Coleman Sears, M.S., "Productive Small Fruit Culture," *Lippincott's Farm Manuals* (Philadelphia: J. B. Lippincott Company, 1920), 146.

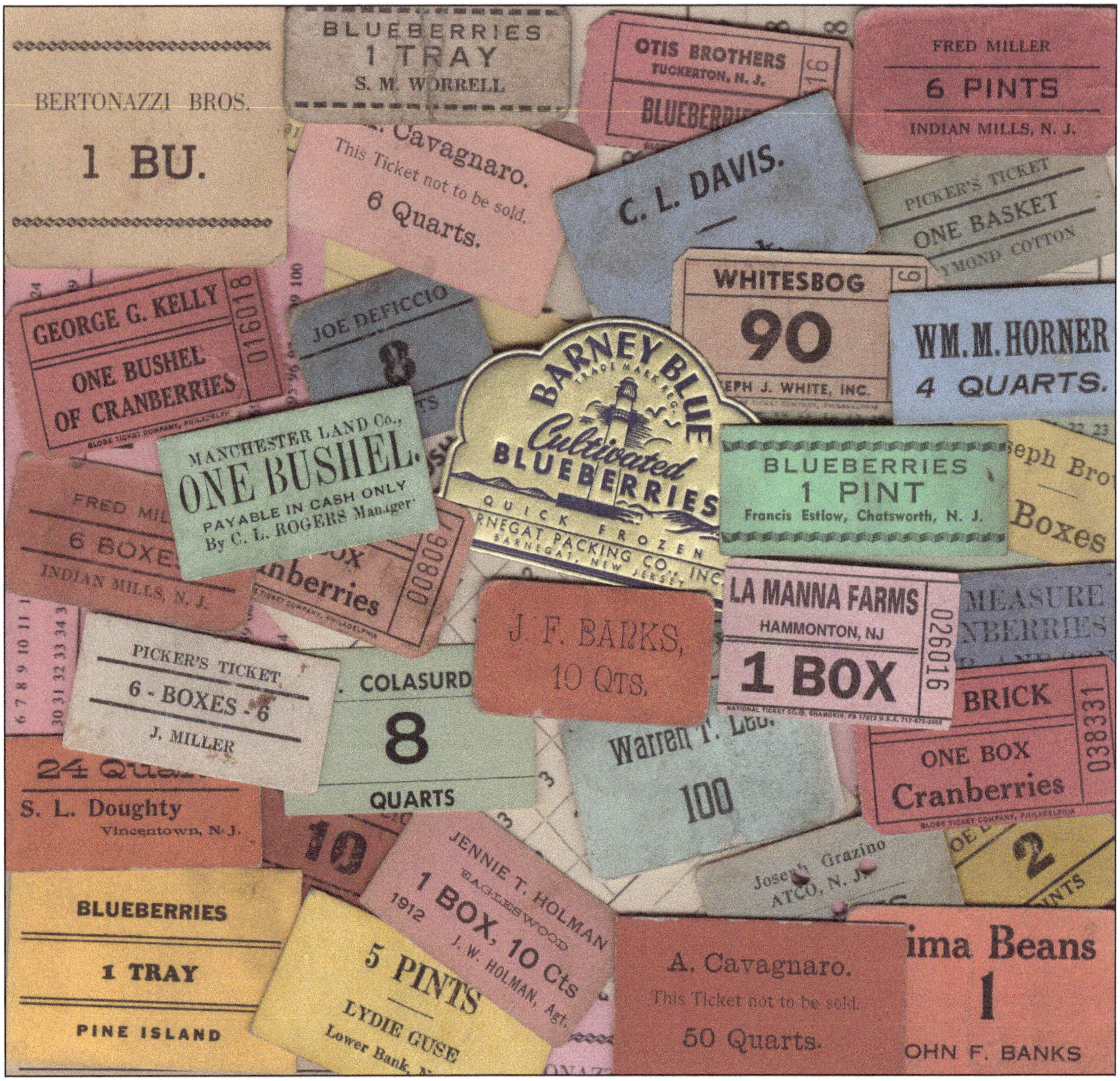

Berry Tickets
the kind you can read, and the kind that lasts,—
Printed by Hoyt & Son

Scooper Tickets Make Your Payoff
SAFE AND EASY

Accurate tickets speed up the work and give you an easy, dependable check on the number of boxes each scooper turns in. Your own name is printed on each ticket for full protection. Write us for complete details.

Globe Ticket Company
112 N. 12th St., Phila., Pa.   113 Albany St., Boston, Mass.

No Use Talking

The EVENING NEWS Office is the place to get your
..STRAWBERRY TICKETS..
printed. We have all the colors of the rainbow and a lot more besides, and the best part of all, the cardboard is a special heavy kind that will last forever, almost. It costs no more to have this sort of strawberry tickets than the cheap, inferior kind.
We are ready to go right ahead with your order next. Bring it along.

Evening News
Fine Job Printing House.

From Butcher Knife to Scalpel:
Four Generations of South Jersey Physicians

Lisa E. Cox, Edward Hutton and Ruth Hutton-Williams

> "Medicine is always the child of its time and cannot escape being influenced and shaped by contemporary ideas and social trends."
> G. Gayle Stephens[1]

> "A son often follows in the footsteps of his father, and occasionally the father had engaged in the same profession as his parent."
> Merritt M. Landon[2]

Charles Butcher, MD, descended from several generations of South Jersey physicians and was himself an esteemed country doctor. The story of the Butcher physicians begins when the family emigrated from England to its American colonies in 1679. Their lives illuminate important aspects of the nineteenth and early twentieth centuries in Cumberland County, New Jersey, and demonstrate how very different life and medicine have become at the start of the twenty-first century.

For six decades, from 1911 until his death in 1976, Dr. Charles Butcher cared for numerous families throughout Maurice River Township and Commercial Township, Cumberland County, New Jersey. He served as the lone physician to the Leesburg Prison Farm population for 57 years, and championed public health issues throughout the region.[3] Children that "Doc" delivered still reside in South Jersey; they are in their 70s, 80s, and 90s now. This is Doc's story, but it is also the story of four generations of physicians in one family, all General Practitioners.

This dynasty of doctors, from eldest to youngest, includes Joseph Butcher the elder, his four sons: Charles Butcher, Joseph Butcher Jr., George E. Butcher, and Samuel Butcher; one grandson, Joseph Butcher; and one great-grandson, Charles "Doc" Butcher. During much of the later nineteenth century, there were three to four Dr. Butchers practicing medicine simultaneously in Cumberland County.

The Butcher family tree stems from England in the 1600s, during the times of Charles I and II, Oliver Cromwell, the Great Plague of London (1665 – 1666), and the persecution of the Religious Society of Friends.[4] This persecution likely led the Butchers to emigrate to Burlington County, like others of their faith.

The authors called Dr. Charles Butcher "Grandpop" and "Uncle Doc." During his lifetime, he served multiple roles as a physician, son, husband, grandfather, uncle, civically active citizen, hunter, farmer and more. His descendants are delighted to reflect back over time and to present his story, along with that of the Butcher doctors who preceded him in the Cumberland County area. Their practices extended along the western edge of Cape May County, New Jersey, with their principal places of residence or offices in Mauricetown, Dividing Creek, and Heislerville, New Jersey—all locations along or proximate to the Maurice River.

The Butchers practiced medicine without the trappings of insurance companies, managed care, HMOs and PPOs, and without advanced technology-based testing procedures, and yet they rendered medical care and treatment to entire families and served their community in vital capacities.

We begin the story with a family heirloom—an excerpt, on the following page, from a printed history describing the medical career of Joseph Butcher, the eldest of the Butcher physicians discussed here. It is found in the 1883 work, *History of the Counties of Gloucester, Salem and Cumberland New Jersey, with Biographical Sketches of Their Prominent Citizens.*

Generations of the Butcher MDs

Joseph Butcher (1791 – 1864). Known as Joseph Jr., Joseph III, and Joseph the elder; the patriarch of this story

SONS of Joseph Butcher the elder and first wife Harriet Elkington

    Charles Butcher (c. 1819 – 1880)
    Joseph Butcher (1824 – 1849)

SONS of Joseph Butcher the elder and Rebecca Cobb

    George Elkington Butcher (1834 – 1904)
    Samuel Butcher (1838 – 1901)

SON of George Elkington Butcher
    Joseph Butcher (1859 – 1918)

SON of Joseph Butcher
    Charles "Doc" Butcher
    (1884 – 1976)

Joseph Butcher (1791 – 1864).

(from *History of the Counties...*)

The Butcher family are of English extraction, Joseph, the father of the subject of this biographical sketch, having resided in Burlington County, where he followed the carpenter's craft, and married Elizabeth Lippincott. Their son Joseph was born May 24, 1791. Port Elizabeth [New Jersey] was the home of his boyhood, the scene of his early educational opportunities, and his later apprenticeship with Israel Stratton to acquire the trade of a tailor. Here he remained for some years, but eventually engaged in mercantile pursuits, and in connection with his partnership supplied a branch of the American army with provisions during the War of 1812. Later he embarked in the drug business, and while thus employed had his attention directed to the study of medicine. He graduated from the Jefferson Medical College[5] at Philadelphia the year of its incorporation, and chose Mauricetown, Cumberland Co., as his first and only field of labor. Here for a period of forty years he continued in active practice, his useful career as a practitioner having ended with his death in August, 1864, in his seventy-fourth year.

Dr. Butcher was thoroughly versed in the science he had espoused, and speedily found that his abilities brought not only reputation, but success. For a long period he controlled the practice of the vicinity, while his steady hand and mature judgment were not less frequently sought during the later years of his life. The doctor during his professional career gave much attention to business pursuits, and for years engaged in farming occupations. He manifested a keen interest in the political events of the day, and invariably espoused the principles of the Democracy. He was, in 1842, elected to the State Legislature, having been the only representative of his party chosen to the position for a long series of years. He also for successive terms held the office of a freeholder, and filled other positions of minor consequence. His thorough knowledge of general law and excellent judgment made his opinion often sought in the settlement of estates as in other matters, and won for him the reputation of a safe and wise counselor. He was an active Odd-Fellow, and a member of the Ariel Lodge, No. 56, of I. O. O. F., of Mauricetown. He was in religion educated in the Quaker faith, but later affiliated with the Methodists. Dr. Butcher was married to Miss Harriet Elkington, of Port Elizabeth, Cumberland Co., and had children who survived,—Rhoda, Ann, Charles, Harriet, William, and Joseph. His wife having died he married again, Miss Rebecca, daughter of Paul and Rhoda Cobb, of Commercial Township. Their children are George E., Eliza (Mrs. Fagan), and Samuel. Mrs. Butcher's death occurred on the 14th of September, 1879. Four sons and a grandson of the doctor have chosen medicine as a profession. Charles graduated at the Pennsylvania College, Philadelphia,[6] and settled in Mauricetown, where he practiced until his decease. Joseph was a graduate of the Jefferson Medical College in 1849, and died at the beginning of his career. George E. graduated from the same college in 1858, and for twenty years continued his professional labors at Dividing Creek, Cumberland Co., subsequently moving to Mauricetown, where he still is active as a practitioner. Samuel received his diploma from the Jefferson Medical College in 1864, and also settled in Mauricetown. Joseph, a son of George E., graduated from the same college in 1883, and is at present assisting his father.[7]

From Butcher Knife to Scalpel

Charles "Doc" Butcher

A year after publication of the tri-county history book quoted here, Charles Butcher was born to Dr. Joseph Butcher. As he matured, Charles graduated from the Heislerville public school system, the South Jersey Institute in Bridgeton (1905), and Jefferson Medical College (1909). The college required Charles to participate in his commencement exercise to obtain his degree of Doctor of Medicine; his diploma named him "*Doctorem in Arte Medendi*." Charles became known as Doc to patients, friends, and family over the course of his long career.

Following graduation, Doc traveled by train to Pueblo, Colorado, to intern at St. Mary's Hospital, first opened in 1882 when the Sisters of Charity converted a two-story boarding house into a hospital. The hospital continues to provide medical care today as the St. Mary-Corwin Medical Center.

Doc's expenses for traveling to Colorado amounted to $82.00, which included a railroad ticket, meals, uniforms, stethoscope and baggage; one night for a sleeper berth cost him $1.50, which provided him with a "double seat all the way to Omaha, Nebraska"; another night he slept in "an upper bunk at a lesser amount," engaging it late at night, "as the amount you paid depended on the distance traveled while it was occupied." At the time, the rail ticket from the East Coast to Colorado cost him $40.85.[8]

By the end of Doc's internship, he had obtained a license from the State of Colorado to practice medicine, and he extended his stay to fill-in for a leading physician who went out of town. This enabled Doc to earn money that he then used to sightsee across the rest of the West prior to returning to New Jersey.

The letters exchanged at this time, between Doc and his father, covered myriad interesting topics. Through them, Doc learned news about his family and South Jersey. Example news items include:

> Regarding the Maurice River fishing industry: "The oyster men started planting last Monday, report planting is good" (May 6, 1910), and the "Blue fish have arrived and fishermen are making good catches. Lewis has a net and he and Rolland are going fishing after school" (May 6, 1910). "The oystermen have started their boats but report that the oysters are in poor condition" (Sept 18, 1910).

> Joseph E.'s horses: "I am having some trouble with my horses again, haven't drove Bell for 10 ds and Cap doesn't seem just himself" (Sept 18, 1910).

> Doc learns that he has a new sister: "Mary, named after her Grand Mother Grace" (Sept 18, 1910).

> In connection to farming in Cumberland County: "I am not doing much farming as yet—Have had the two first pieces of the meadow plowed—It was getting so foul that I had to have it broken up. I intend to put corn there myself," and "We had a very mild Mar, and I was enabled to plant some early garden. We have peas, beans, cabbage, potatoes all growing nicely; have had radishes for some time. Rolland planted some lima beans about 3 or 4 weeks before any one else thought of doing so, I told him that He would have to set up nights with them, but I haven't heard of his loosing [*sic*] any sleep on account of them" (May 6, 1910).

In letters to his father, Doc chatted about his patients in Pueblo, Colorado:

Young Doc and sister Priscilla. *All images courtesy of the authors unless otherwise specified.*

Doc (at left) out West.

1910, Doc settled in Heislerville, his hometown, located in Maurice River Township. He obtained a license to practice Medicine and Surgery in the State of New Jersey (license No. 3132), issued July 5, 1911. Doc began practice and saw patients both in their homes and in his office. He also served as consulting physician at the State Prison Farm. He drove a Model-T Ford in the summer, and a horse and buggy in the winter.

Doc was the first Butcher physician to own and use an automobile for house calls. The receipt below, for a 1919 Ford Sedan costing $836.57, shows that he purchased this car from Gus C. Westcott of 608 High Street, Millville, New Jersey. Doc, who was quite a storyteller, explained that when the weather was rainy, cold, or snowy, he might leave the Ford at home and use the horse and carriage or sleigh. During good and bad weather, if you needed Doc's help, you tied a towel or cloth on the front porch and the horse knew to stop. After one particularly wet, cold day, however, while nearing home, food, and shelter, the horse saw a towel and took off for home, not wanting to stand waiting in the cold while Doc made his last call. Doc reined in his cold, wet, and hungry horse, and returned to the house that needed help.

Additional interesting receipts from Doc's practice include a receipt for hospital visit and delivery of a baby girl (this was Eleanor Butcher-Hutton, mother of two of the co-authors) at Millville Hospital in June 1917. The birth took place on June 15, and the cost for a fifteen-day hospital stay was $34.30; an additional delivery room charge of $5.00 made the total $39.30. Though Doc delivered any number of babies at patients' homes, and Doc's own birth certificate shows his birth occurred at home (with his father as attending physician), Doc's daughters were all born in a hospital.

"There was a case of Leukemia came in a few days ago. I examined his blood this morning and found his white blood cells were about 8 times as numerous as they should be. The doctors have not had any one here for a long time who would examine blood or do that kind of work, so they appreciate it very much.

Last evening Tinker and I went down to one of the doctor's offices [and] examined a fellow from the hospital with the X-ray. After we had gone over the patient, the doctor invited us out to the dining room to have some watermelon. So we had an interesting and enjoyable time. We did not find out very much with the X-ray. But doctor is going to do an exploration on him Tuesday" (August 29, 1909).[9]

Having returned from his medical training at the end of

From Butcher Knife to Scalpel

At the start of Doc's 1917 – 1925 account book, he charged $0.50 for an office visit and $1.00 for a house call. In 1918 – 1919, Doc upped the price, charging $1.25 for a house call, between $2.50 – $5.00 to set a fracture, and anywhere between $0.50 – $1.00 for medicine. A close examination of this account book suggests that payment for medical care was generally tendered after the fact. Bills were allowed to accumulate and then collected in a batch during the summer or fall, and, sometimes, across years. Family members speculate that Doc offered his patients credit until after harvest or for other reasons. For example, the account book contains instances where bills accumulated from July through October, and then he received cash payments of $20.00 and $30.00. In another case, for services rendered from October through the following March, he received a check in the amount of $70.50 in May. Yet another example of Doc's services from December 1915 to October 13, 1918, totaled $29.00, and he accepted a check for that amount on January 25, 1919.

Life along the Maurice River

The Maurice River (pronounced "Morris") was named for the Dutch ship Prins Maurits, which unexpectedly grounded on a sandbar during a voyage in 1657, not far from present day Mauricetown. Settled in the early 1700s, the region "blossomed at the turn of the subsequent century, when watermen began to harvest a wealth of oysters." Good times on the river continued through the 1920s, but then the Great Depression stifled wealth and shortly thereafter World War II took the men away. In 1956, the microscopic parasite, dubbed MSX, killed the oysters.[10]

In 1989, Mauricetown contained about 300 people and 120 homes, most of them Victorian and stately, built by wealthy sea captains who left them in neglect when the sea no longer provided their affluency. Today, in 2016, these Victorian homes have been "found" again. Most are adorned with bright paint and wear plaques detailing their origin: Dr. Joseph Butcher, 1799, George Fagan, 1853, J. Milton Compton, 1880. Mauricetown's small historical society conducts tours of the town, with the most popular tour being at Christmas time.[11]

One such home on the tour is The Elkinton-Butcher House. This home is a two and a half story, double-pile, side passage, federal-style brick dwelling. The home's south façade has three bay windows, to which a subsequent owner appended a twentieth-century screen porch. George Elkinton built this private residence sometime during the late eighteenth or early nineteenth century, and he is believed to have lived in this house with his wife, Beulah Elkinton, until his death in 1820. In 1846, Dr. Joseph Butcher the elder formally acquired the property.[12]

The Previous Three Generations Living and Practicing Medicine along the Maurice River

First Generation

The earliest Butcher physician referenced in this article is Joseph Butcher (1791 – 1864), variously and confusingly named Joseph III, Joseph Jr., and Joseph "the elder." In this article he is referred to as Joseph the elder. He received his medical degree in 1826 as a member of the first graduating class of Jefferson Medical College in Philadelphia. Joseph owned medical texts, preserved by family members, with provenance dating from 1814 and 1815, predating his professional training at Jefferson. Typical of the time and place, he combined subsistence, agricultural, political, and commercial pursuits with his medical practice. He was a tailor, storeowner, druggist (including sales of liquor), and, later in life, an elected member of the State Legislature, a judge of the Court of Common Pleas, a township freeholder, and a justice of the peace.[13]

Joseph the elder's account book from the 1830s records, among other items, the purchase of a horse in 1839. Records of timber, cut and sold, figure prominently: cords of pine and oak wood cut and sold from Bailey Field in 1830, 1831, and 1838 (totaling several hundred cords); purchase of timber from three lots at John Cobb's sale for $121.05; and more wood cutting, possibly for cord wood sales at the Buckshutum store.

Joseph the elder's Buckshutum general store was probably located along Buckshutum Road near the mill in Commercial Township, Cumberland County. Among its varied merchandise, the store sold cordwood, and also butter, flower, molasses, coffee, mutton, fish, candles, shoes, cotton cloth, scissors, brooms, powder and shot, rum, and an occasional purchase of gin.

A store account book from this period records the price of a half-gallon of rum as $0.25; the price for the same volume of molasses was identical. A pound of sugar was $0.13, two pounds of coffee $0.34, and three half-dozen cartons of eggs were $0.35. On November 15, 1833, a Richard Mitchel received $5.00 in cash as a loan, six pounds of coffee at $0.17 per pound ($1.02), six pounds of sugar ($0.66), one pound of tea ($1.13), six pounds of candy at $0.14 per pound ($0.84), three yards of calico at 12.5 cents per yard ($0.38), for a total debt of $9.03. It is likely that Joseph loaned cash, and allowed store items on credit, to be paid at a later time. Debits and credits appear throughout the book. Also, empty bottles sold for 12.5 cents, so if you needed a bottle for that quart of rum the cost became $0.25 instead of $0.13.

Following the 65-page store account book is a twelve-page index of patients, in alphabetical order, with reference to the following 184 pages of medical accounts listing debits for services and credits for payments.

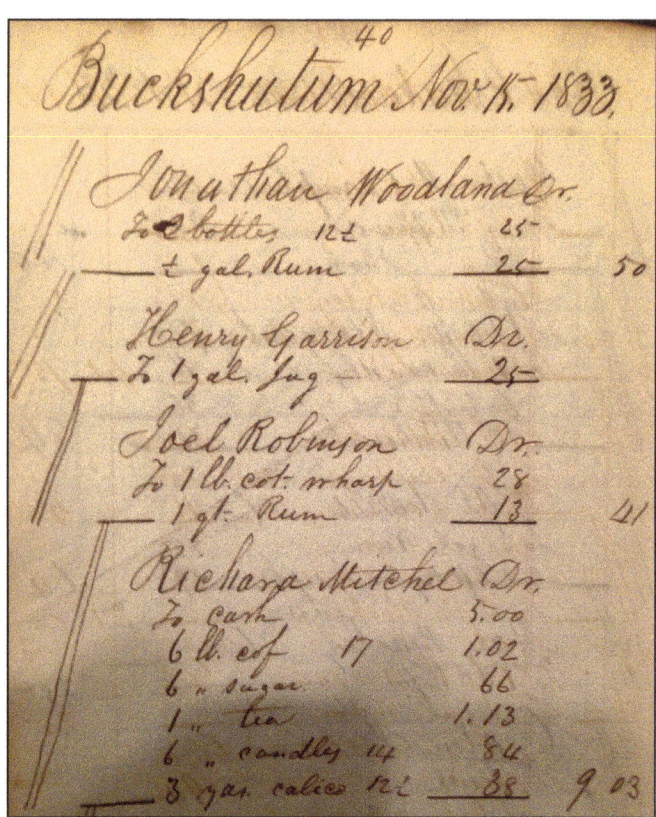

Page from Buckshutum account book, November 15, 1833.

The account for Mr. William J. Campbell, from the listing under C and D in the client index, spreads across two pages: the left leaf is for debits and the right for credits. During October 1834, Joseph Butcher the elder paid a medical visit to the daughter and son of Campbell: visit and medicine totaled of $3.00. The account continues for March 1836, for four visits with medicine, and then into the summer of 1837 for visits and more medicine. Including a $3.00 balance carried from another page, the total for Mr. Campbell was $10.75. The credit side carries over a $9.00 balance to a second book after a credit of $1.75 is shown for receipt of three and a half bushels of oysters at $0.50 per bushel, during March 1836. The oysters were likely soon sold in the Buckshutum store.

Second Generation

Charles Butcher (c. 1819 – 1880), the son of Joseph Butcher the elder and his first wife, Harriet Elkington, graduated from the Pennsylvania College, Philadelphia (now the University of Pennsylvania), and settled in Mauricetown, where he practiced medicine until his death. In 1846 he ran on the Democratic ticket as coroner for Downe Township, Cumberland County, and held that position as late as 1878.[14] He was a participant in the 1848 revival of the District Medical Society of Cumberland County. Originally organized in 1818, this local society was active until 1830, "at which time it is said that there were so few who attended its meetings or manifested any interest in its proceedings, that it became extinct."[15] Charles and colleagues (including his father) reinvigorated the society. Like his brothers and father, Charles was involved with the local Odd Fellows and was elected as Cumberland County district deputy for that organization in 1851.[16] Charles was elected as freeholder in the Township of Downe, Cumberland County, succeeding his father, in 1860 – 1861, and again in 1871 – 1873; he was appointed justice of the peace for Cumberland County in 1877.[17] He ran for state assembly several times on the Democratic ticket.

Joseph Butcher Jr. (1824 – 1849), the son of Joseph Butcher the elder and Harriet Elkington, was born in Mauricetown, on March 10, 1824. He graduated from the Jefferson Medical College of Philadelphia, in the class of 1848 – 1849, and died approximately six months later on October 17, 1849.

The following preamble and resolutions were adopted at a special meeting of Ariel Lodge, No. 56, Independent Order of Odd Fellows:

> WHEREAS, It has pleased the Almighty, in the mysterious workings of his Providence, to cut down in the Spring time of his years, and the opening of his manhood, just as he was prepared for a useful life, our well-beloved brother, Dr. Joseph Butcher, Jr. therefore
>
> Resolved, That we the officers and members of his own Lodge, and sister Lodges, feel with deep and heart-felt sensibility the loss sustained by our Order, and the community in which he resided.
>
> Resolved, That in his death we have lost a brother endeared to us by his pure life and worthy example, and humanity has cause to mourn the departure of a sterling friend.[18]

George E. Butcher (1834 – 1904) is another representative of the second generation of Butcher physicians. He was the son of Joseph Butcher the elder and his second wife, Rebecca Cobb. George E. graduated from medical school in 1858 and spent most of his career practicing medicine in Dividing Creek. Newspaper accounts suggest that he moved his practice to Mauricetown following his brother Samuel's death in 1901.[19]

George E. applied himself until the end, as a contemporary newspaper reports:

> Tuesday night [December 13, 1904] Dr. George E. Butcher was summoned to Haleyville at 10 o'clock. When about a mile from home he said to his driver, "I am very sick; stop at the first house you see a light in." They stopped at Henry Robbins'. Dr. Butcher took off his coat and sat down and asked for a doctor and died within one minute.[20]

From Butcher Knife to Scalpel

George E. Butcher.

George E. assembled a fascinating 200-page recipe book that includes recipes for a wide range of ailments—from diarrhea and headaches to whooping cough. These recipes include ingredients for ginger beer and treatments for cholera.

Samuel Butcher (1838 - 1901) was the youngest child of Joseph the elder and Rebecca Cobb. He remained at the house in Mauricetown with his mother and continued the practice established there first by Joseph the elder, then by Charles, his brother. A newspaper report in March 1895 describes Samuel's work:

> There is much sickness in our community. Miss A. E. Prichard, one of our school teachers, has been confined to the house nearly a week, but is now better. Many children are also sick. Dr. Samuel Butcher has been very busy for the last two weeks.[21]

Like his brothers and father, Samuel was a member of the International Order of Odd Fellows, Ariel Lodge, No. 56. In 1895, he prepared and delivered a lecture on the history of this lodge, noting that it was instituted on July 8, 1848, with his father Joseph and brother Charles among its charter members.[22] Samuel remained in the Butcher-Elkington House in Mauricetown until his death in 1901, continuing to maintain two front rooms as space for medical supplies and receiving and examining patients.[23] His death, reported in the *Bridgeton Evening News*, "was the direct result of a stroke of paralysis with which he was afflicted recently while addressing a lodge of the Odd Fellows."[24] The grave memorial for Samuel, in the Methodist church burial ground at Haleyville, Cumberland County, reads: "Worth ever its own reward, here finds its appreciation in grateful hearts. He will always live in the memory of the many he helped."

Third Generation

Joseph Butcher (May 17, 1859 – August 3, 1918), representing the third generation of Butcher physicians, was born to George E. and Priscilla Joslyn Butcher. When Joseph graduated from Jefferson in 1883, he

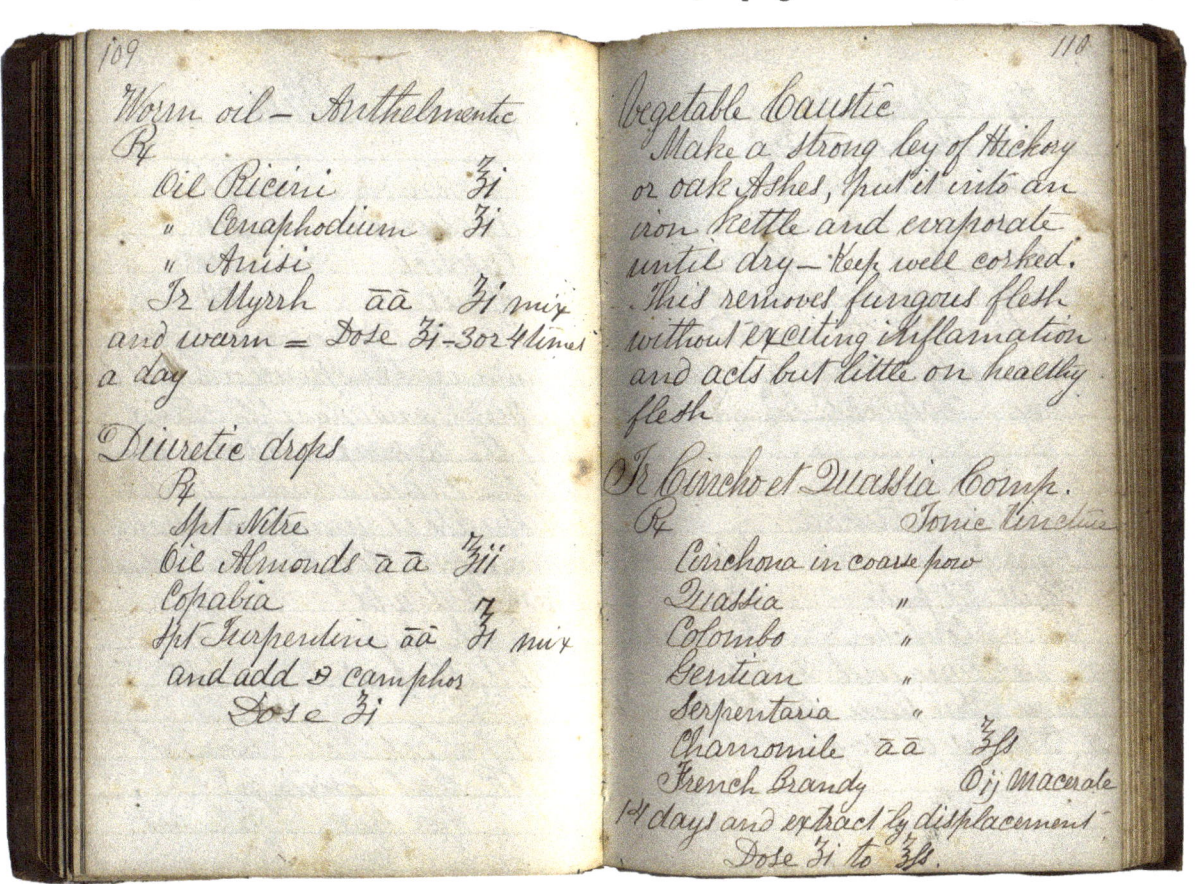

At first glance, the toned pages of George Butcher's recipe book are a challenge to read: the ingredients are obscure and quantities are difficult to interpret. Nevertheless, this book provides excellent examples of types of treatments used in the 1800s.

became the fourth Cumberland County Butcher to have received his training there, which had not yet reached its sixtieth year of incorporation. He married Beulah Elliott Ludlam Butcher (1858 – 1898), and had four children, including Doc Butcher, their eldest, while building a large practice in Heislerville. In addition to his active medical practice, for several years he served on the Board of Education for Maurice River Township.[25] Beulah Butcher died in 1898 and in 1909 the *Bridgeton Evening News* announced "Physician Takes Bride."[26] Joseph married Deborah Eletha Grace and they had a daughter, Mary Butcher. In July 1917, little more than three months after the United States declared war against Germany, Joseph was actively engaged in organizing a Red Cross Auxiliary in Heislerville.[27] Joseph died on August 3, 1918.

Doc Finishes His Career

Doc did not believe that members of his direct family line were the only Butchers to have entered the medical profession. In addition to the Butchers of Cumberland County, an index of Jefferson graduates from 1826 – 1890, lists two Pennsylvanians: a Henry B. Butcher as a graduate in 1866 and a Thomas S. Butcher, as a graduate in 1868, suggesting that the extended Butcher family practiced medicine in Pennsylvania as well as in South Jersey. A James Butcher is referenced in 1846, practicing as an MD in Mauricetown, alongside Joseph the Elder.[28]

Family lore also suggests that Joseph the elder was not the first Butcher physician. Evidence indicates that Joseph Butcher I (1728 – 1818), grandfather to Joseph the elder, was a physician. Doc Butcher described an even earlier ancestor, a doctor in England, who invented one of the early instruments that later evolved into a physician's scalpel. Naturally, they dubbed it "The Butcher Knife."

Doc's career was long and productive, and, near its conclusion, garnered its share of honors. A second heirloom of the Butcher descendants is a "Thank You Speech" Doc prepared. It may date to 1959, when the Medical Society of New Jersey presented him with the Golden Merit Award for fifty years of distinguished service as a practicing physician, or he may have penned it in 1954, at the time of a testimonial dinner honoring him for serving twenty-two years as the president of the Cumberland County Tuberculosis and Health Association.[29] He also served as president of the Cumberland County Medical Society during 1940 – 1941, as had his grandfather George E., 50 years prior.

As part of the speech, Doc told the story of a surgeon speaking at a banquet many years earlier at Jefferson Medical College. The last half of the nineteenth century, asserted the speaker, showed more medical advancement than any other like period in the history of man.[30] In 1732 in England, the speaker stated, a newborn had a fifty-percent chance of surviving to its second birthday.

Joseph E. Butcher.

By the early twentieth century, vast improvements had been achieved. Doc reminded his audience that at the mid-point of the twentieth century "smallpox, diphtheria, tuberculosis and typhoid fever have been practically annihilated or brought under control during the last two or three decades." Doc noted that "Medicine continues to advance and as it does it becomes more complicated. In looking through my P.D.I., a book that lists items of most American pharmaceutical houses, I was struck by the number of remedies for one general disease, dermatitis. There were 354."[31]

What would Doc think today? Anesthesiology was only coming in to use during the middle of the nineteenth century with little universal use until the twentieth century. When Doc began caring for patients, insulin, vitamin pills, tranquilizers and antibiotics were not available. Joseph Butcher, Doc's father, wrote his 1883 thesis on peritonitis, a dangerous and uncomfortable inflammation of the tissues that line the inner wall of the abdomen. The care at the time was patient rest and limited eating to "keep bowels quiet and [with] no peristaltic action." To check exertion, "nothing equals opium or alkaloid morphia (morphine)—one or two grains for first dose and one-half grain every hour or two thereafter." In addition, "bloodletting may be productive or beneficial (either general or local) within 24 hours and a hot or cold compress to the abdomen to provide comfort."[32] X-rays were discovered when Doc was eleven years old. Clearly much medical progress had been made during his lifetime.[33]

By the time Doc passed away in 1976, he had maintained his right to practice medicine for nearly seventy years. The Medical Society of New Jersey acknowledged his more than fifty years of service. He had completed fifty-seven years, from 1913 to 1970, "ministering to the physical needs of the inmates of the Leesburg Prison Farm,"[34] and he had contributed numerous hours to local medical associations as well as serving as a member of the Maurice River Township School Board. Like his antecedents, he combined family, medicine, community service, and hobbies into an active life. Returning to his "Thank You Speech," Doc observed that, "if we cannot look forward to gratify some whim of a hobby, to maintain some cultural advancement in music or art, anticipate a good book, relish the prospect of fraternizing with kindred spirits, and planning to be of some service to our fellow man—we are irretrievably lost." Quoting Chauncey DePew, he also offered the advice that "as one advances in years he should try to do most of the things he had been accustomed to doing but do a little less of them."

In what seems an eerily appropriate conclusion, he remarked,

> It seems as we delve into the cause of many diseases we find ourselves searching farther down the scale of life to the viruses and yeast-like organisms, even to the atom itself, and in this approach we take a glimpse at creativity. May we hope that this directional trend will not take us toward war but nearer our creator by the reduction of pestilence and disease.

Was Doc anticipating undiscovered viral diseases, the investigation of yeast and health, and the development of genetically modified organisms? Certainly, he was hoping for the best for humanity.

Afterword

While preparing this article about four generations of South Jersey physicians, thoughts came to mind about the current state-of-affairs regarding medical practice today. Of particular interest is an article entitled "Primary Care Docs: Only 15% Happy with US Healthcare System." It found that "As a nation we are spending far too much time on insurance, with each insurer asking for different reports and using different drug formularies and adopting different payment methods—we need to stop draining resources and redirect it for care."[37]

We also noted that Malcolm Gladwell on *Telling the Story of Medicine* said,

---

Some of Doc's Expenses[35]

Expenses Doc incurred on September 25, 1905, while in medical training at Jefferson Hospital in Philadelphia, Pennsylvania:

Tuition: $185.00 (an increase from the 1856 – 1857 session fee of $105.00)
Board: $4.75 weekly (no mention of where)
Alarm clock: $0.75
Shirt: $1.00
Whisky: $0.15
Haircut: $0.20
Museum: $0.10
Peanuts: $0.05

Expenses at the beginning of 1906:

Trip home: $2.25 (no mention of method)
Boxing gloves: $1.45
Valentines: $0.67
Stamps: $0.20
Ferry: $0.05
Trolley: $0.13
Beggar: $0.05
Theater: $3.00 (we would love to know what was featured at this time)
Moving pictures: $0.30
Union suit: $1.50

"I remember talk of while at Jefferson Grandpop attended a show of Houdini. He was called on stage to check Houdini's chains."[36]

> . . . the world of healthcare does a very bad job of storytelling about itself . . . the gap between the reality of medicine and the way the public thinks about medicine is growing, not shrinking. . . . What is so striking when you talk to ordinary, front-line doctors is how frustrated and unhappy they are in the present day with the way that their workloads have shifted, how their status in society has changed, and the way that electronic medical records have been conceived and pushed on them so that their own interests are last. That is a classic storytelling problem.[38]

The stories told about medicine through the lives of the Butcher physicians, from the late 1700s through 1976 are quite different. They practiced medicine with compassion and careful assessment; they accepted payment when it was available; and they involved themselves as intimate participants in community life. At the same time, they enjoyed life—work and play—along the Maurice River. The Butcher physicians have left a memorable and significant legacy that attests to their integrity, citizenry, aptitude for learning, and rendering of fine medical care during a time that cared not about insurance, electronic records or quality assurance.

Endnotes

Lisa Cox, PhD, L.C.S.W., M.S.W., graduated from Virginia Commonwealth University with a Doctorate in Social Work and Social Policy and is Professor of Social Work & Gerontology at Stockton University where she teaches undergraduate and graduate level students. Dr. Cox's expertise is in clinical and health social work and gerontology and her roots are in South Jersey. Lisa was born and raised in Cumberland County, New Jersey (Maurice River Township). Her father was named Joseph Butcher Cox Sr., and her Grammy was Mary Butcher Cox—a sister to "Uncle Doc"—and daughter of Joseph Butcher, MD, and Deborah Grace-Butcher. Lisa's mother (Joyce Cox-Meyh age 77), Aunt Eileen (age 84), and Uncle Don (age 67) were all delivered by "Doc" at home in Delmont, NJ (Maurice River Township).

Edward Hutton, PhD, M.S., holds a Doctorate in Economics from the University of Rhode Island. Dr. Hutton is retired Deputy Director of the Medicare Demonstrations Program Group, within the Center for Medicare and Medicaid Innovation at the Centers for Medicare & Medicaid Services. "Doc" was Ed's Grandpop. Ed has a twin brother Charlie, a younger brother John and a sister Ruth. Ed's mom, Eleanor, was daughter of "Doc" and niece of Mary Butcher Cox.

Ruth Hutton-Williams resides in North Carolina where she worked for 26 years in textile design and operated a yarn shop. She received a B.S. in Textile Design from Philadelphia College of Textiles and Design (1981) renamed Philadelphia University. (This year—2016—Jefferson and Philadelphia University have joined, so Ruth, in a way, graduated from the same school as all of our Dr. grands!)

Doc Butcher.

From Butcher Knife to Scalpel

Lisa, Ed and Ruth are cousins. They have fond memories of spending happy family times in South Jersey and hearing stories about their distinguished grandparents and relatives.

1. G. Gayle Stephens, *The Intellectual Basis of Family Practice* (Tucson, AZ: Winter Publishing Co., 1982).
2. Merritt M. Landon, *The Press of Atlantic City*, Staff Writer, 1962.
3. The Leesburg Prison farm, located in Leesburg, Maurice River Township, Cumberland County, was renamed Bayside State Prison in 1988.
4. The Society of Friends, also known as Quakers, arrived in South Jersey (then known as West Jersey) in 1677, several years before they arrived in the better-known Quaker stronghold of Philadelphia.
5. Now the Sidney Kimmel Medical College of Thomas Jefferson University.
6. The Medical School of the College of Philadelphia was founded in 1765. The College of Philadelphia and University of the State of Pennsylvania merged in 1791, forming the University of Pennsylvania.
7. From Thomas Cushing, MD, and Charles E. Sheppard, Esq, *History of the Counties of Gloucester, Salem and Cumberland New Jersey, with Biographical Sketches of Their Prominent Citizens* (Philadelphia: Everts & Peck, 1883), 562-63.
8. These details derive from records kept by family members.
9. These details derive from letters kept by family members.
10. Joe Daly, "Renewing a Heritage of Life on the River along The Maurice in South Jersey, the Boats Return, Laden with Life," Special to *The Inquirer* (Philadelphia), August 11, 1989, 1. http://articles.philly.com/1989-08-11/entertainment/26150285_1_river-today-oysters-fishing p. 2.
11. Maurice River Township Heritage Society: To apply, mail to Maurice River Township Heritage Society, P.O. Box 195 Leesburg, NJ 08327.
12. Deed of Sale from George E. Wills to Joseph Butcher, May 20, 1846, Cumberland County, New Jersey, Deed Book 76, page 8. Recorder of Deeds. Bridgeton, New Jersey.
13. Joseph the elder was elected to the State Legislature in 1842; see Cushing and Sheppard, *History of the Counties*, 563. He was appointed judge in 1836, see Cushing and Sheppard, 533; and also *New Jersey, Leglislature, Journal of the Proceedings of the Legislative-Council of the State of New-Jersey* (Somerville, NJ: Gore & Allinson, 1836), 25. He was appointed justice of the peace in 1832, 1837. His son George E. was appointed justice of the peace in 1875, 1880, and 1882; and his son Charles was appointed justice of the peace in 1877: see Cushing and Sheppard, 534-35. Joseph the elder was a member of the board of freeholders from the township of Downe, Cumberland County, in 1832 – 42, 1846 – 59: see Cushing and Sheppard, 660.
14. *Bridgeton Chronicle* (Bridgeton, NJ), October 31, 1846, 5. *Trenton State Gazette* (Trenton, NJ), September 9, 1878, 2.
15. Cushing and Sheppard, *History of the Counties*, 571.
16. *Newark Daily Advertiser* (Newark, NJ), August 9, 1851, 2.
17. Cushing and Sheppard, *History of the Counties*, 535, 660.
18. *Transactions of the Medical Society of New Jersey* (Newark, NJ: Jennings & Hardham, 1871), 159-60.
19. *Bridgeton Evening News* (Bridgeton, NJ), February 1, 1905, 3. Cushing and Sheppard, however, suggest that George E. moved his practice from Dividing Creek to Mauricetown at least by 1883.
20. *Bridgeton Evening News* (Bridgeton, NJ), December 15, 1904, 2.
21. *Bridgeton Evening News* (Bridgeton, NJ), March 8, 1895, 2.
22. *Bridgeton Evening News* (Bridgeton, NJ), July 12, 1895, 2.
23. Wikipedia, The Free Encyclopedia, "Elkington-Butcher House" Accessed June 1, 2016) https://en.m.wikipedia.org/wiki/Elkinton-Butcher_House.
24. *Bridgeton Evening News* (Bridgeton, NJ), October 17, 1901, 4.
25. *Bridgeton Evening News* (Bridgeton, NJ), August 16, 1907, 1 and *Bridgeton Evening News* (Bridgeton, NJ), July 27, 1914, 2.
26. *Bridgeton Evening News* (Bridgeton, NJ), December 14, 1909, 3.
27. *Bridgeton Evening News* (Bridgeton, NJ), July 16, 1917, 3.
28. Lorenzo F. Lee first began advertising in the *Bridgeton Chronicle* on May 28, 1842. He was a clock and watchmaker. By June 29, 1844, he is advertising as a dentist, "having received a course of instruction from an experienced Dentist in Philadelphia" (although he still repaired clocks). By May 23, 1846, his advertisement includes a list of references from nine local physicians, including Joseph Butcher the elder, MD, and James Butcher, MD, both of Mauricetown. *Bridgeton Chronicle* (Bridgeton, NJ), May 28, 1842; June 29, 1844; and May 23, 1846.
29. Awards & Programs left by Doc; Cushing and Sheppard, *History of the Counties*, 572.
30. This was the HARE Honor Society banquet hosted by Professor of Therapeutics Hobart Amory Hare, date c. 1908.
31. P.D.I. probably stands for a physician's drug index such as the *Merck Index of Chemicals and Drugs An Encyclopedia for the Chemist, Pharmacist, Physician, and Allied Professions*. It is related to the modern physician's desk reference.
32. Joseph Butcher, "An Inaugural Dissertation on Peritonitis," submitted to the Faculty of the Jefferson Medical College of Philadelphia for the degree of Doctor of Medicine, February 1883. In the possession of family members.
33. "Roentgen's Discover of X-Rays," *APS News* 10.10 (November 2001), accessed October 3, 2016, https://www.aps.org/publications/apsnews/200111/history.cfm.
34. State Board of Control of Institutions & Agencies [New Jersey], "Letter of recognition to Charles Butcher, MD," July 22, 1970. In the possession of family members.
35. This material is derived from paperwork held by Doc's granddaughter, Ruth Hutton-Williams.
36. Personal Communication from Ruth Hutton-Williams, granddaughter of Charles Butcher.
37. Emma Hitt, PhD, published online November 16, 2012, in *Health Affairs*. Information derives from a Commonwealth Fund International Health Policy Survey: the survey gathered responses from 8,462 primary care physicians in

ten countries including the U.S., accessed November 16, 2012, http://www.medscape.com/viewarticle/774582_print.

38 Eric J. Topol and Malcolm Gladwell, "Telling the Story of Medicine," *Medscape*, accessed Aug 4, 2015, http://www.medscape.com/viewarticle/847713_print.

Independence Day Program, Woodbury, New Jersey, 1943. Men and women were joining the military in unprecedented numbers as the Second World War dragged on for the United States. Nineteen months into the global conflict, the City of Woodbury, New Jersey, held its annual Independence Day celebration, complete with an amazing full-color program. Patriotism was at a fever pitch and most Americans had hearts swelled with national pride. The program cover reflects these themes using the iconography of the period: the bald eagle; a shield based on the American flag overlaying a similarly designed "V" for victory. Dignitaries and ordinary citizens filed into the high school auditorium that evening, while the Cedar Concert Orchestra tuned up, waiting to play a number of Sousa marches. A quartet from Boy Scout Troop 51 prepared to sing a special patriotic number in four-part harmony. Officials provided the usual obligatory rousing speeches and those in attendance who came to hear the presentations of music and the spoken word bonded together as prideful Americans bound with a single unity of purpose: to defeat malevolent evil and win the war and bring the G.I.s back home to their families. The war would drag on for over two more years before the hopes and dreams of those Woodbury residents would be realized.

Manufacturing from Menhaden:

A History in the Mullica Valley

Kenneth W. Able

The menhaden is a fish with numerous names: frequently bunker, often pogy, mossbunker, hardhead, oldwife, or greentail, depending on locality, time period and stage of maturation.[1] The fish frequents the ocean, estuaries and bays all along the east coast of the United States, including the Mullica Valley. The adult fish spawn in the ocean and the eggs and early larvae are found there, but the developing larvae find their way into estuaries, where they transform into juveniles that are often referred to as peanuts or peanut bunker.

Both Native Americans and early colonists harvested menhaden for use as guano fertilizer. The history of the commercial menhaden fisheries began with the discovery that these fish produced a high-quality oil when boiled, providing a fuel for lamps and other purposes. The demand for this oil increased dramatically when whale oil, the mainstay of the lamp and fuel industry, became less available due to overfishing during the nineteenth century. Over time, and especially during the twentieth century, the list of products manufactured from menhaden grew from guano fertilizer to a whole host of uses, including the attempt to portray it as a human food (Fig. 1, Table 1).

Early colonists caught the fish with small nets in shallow waters, but as the interests in the various products grew, the fisheries expanded into deeper waters to capture the large oceangoing schools of menhaden with sail and then steam-powered vessels. The recorded landings increased from the 1940s to a peak in the late 1950s and early 1960s but declined after that (Fig. 2). This decline was most obvious north of Chesapeake Bay, where the adults became scarce. Since the 1980s, when records began to be kept, the landings for the bait fisheries (primarily for lobster, crab and hook and line) have increased up to the present. During the same period, the landings for reducing fish into a variety of products were at recorded lows (Fig. 2). The products of reduction included fishmeal, fish oil, and fish solubles.

Of particular interest in the Mullica Valley, and elsewhere the fisheries existed, Joseph Wharton of Philadelphia played a major role in modernizing the industry. Wharton maintained varied interests throughout the Pine Barrens from agriculture to the aquifer. He invested in the Crab Island menhaden fishery as early as the mid-1890s. He then extended his interests to New England and bought several offshore steam-powered fishing vessels equipped with purse seines, a new technique that used two boats and a large net to surround the menhaden schools.

In the early 1900s, Wharton began several efforts to consolidate the menhaden fishery through the acquisition of other fishing vessels, and eventually forming the Wharton Fisheries Company. By 1906, Wharton owned menhaden fisheries stretching from New England to

Fig. 1. Business card of James E. Otis, who attempted to portray Atlantic menhaden as food for humans.

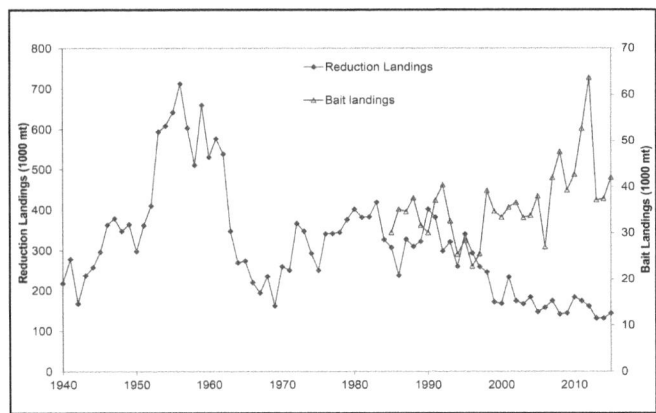

Fig. 2. Annual landings of Atlantic menhaden from the reduction purse seine fishery (1940 – 2015) and bait fishery (1985 – 2015) along the east coast of the U.S. *Atlantic States Marine Fisheries Commission*.

Table 1. *Some uses for processed menhaden over time, including some of the earliest (lamp oils) to a variety of industrial uses.*

Attractant and Lures
Lubricants and Greases
Automotive Gaskets
Mold-Release Agents
Caulking Compounds
Mushroom Culture
Ceramic Deflocculants
Oil-Field Chemicals
Core Oils
Oiled Fabrics
Cutting Oils
Ore Flotation
Fatty Acids
Plasticizers
Fatty Chemicals
Polyurethane Lures
Fermentation Substrates
Presswood Fiber Boards
Fire Retardants
Printing Inks
Lamp Oils
Fuel Oils
Protective Coatings
Glazing Compounds
Refractory Compounds
Rustproofing
Insecticidal Compounds
Soaps
Leather Tanning
Specialty Chemicals
Linoleum
Tin-Plating Oils

Modified from the *Virginia Marine Research Bulletin* (1994).

the east coast and in the Mullica Valley (Fig. 4). Another critical issue was locating the factories a proper distance from human population centers due to the strong smells emanating from the soft oily fish as they decayed and/or underwent processing. Thus, the local name for the fish factories, stink houses or stink factories, still survives today. Other characteristics of these factories were frequent changes in ownership or leaseholder, and frequent catastrophic, destructive fires. As a result, only a paucity of information exists concerning the history of individual factories. What we do know provides fascinating insights into these very important fisheries.

The earliest factory in the Mullica Valley started in 1868 on Wells Island near Turtle Island on upper Great Bay (Fig. 3, 4). This fishery remained in operation until circa 1880, but virtually no documentation exists for the plant. The same applies to two other factories that stood in the Sheepshead Meadows (formerly called the Fox Boroughs or Burrows on some older maps) along Marshelder Channel just north of Big Sheepshead Creek (Fig. 4). The first and most northerly of these factories, dating to 1871, appears on some maps as a "guano" factory because the plant produced fertilizer from the menhaden at that time. The second factory, located immediately to the south, began as a separate operation, but some evidence exists that these two operations merged sometime during the late 1870s. They continued to operate until the early 1890s.

South Carolina. These included 41 steam-powered fishing vessels and eight processing factories for making fish oil and fertilizer and employed about 2,600 people.[2]

Fish Factories in the Mullica Valley

The history of the menhaden fisheries—the how, where and when of these activities—is largely mirrored in the history of the Mullica Valley fish factories from the 1890s until today (Fig. 3). They all shared several characteristics: among the most important was access to deep water for the larger boats involved in the offshore purse seine fishing that soon became the mainstay along

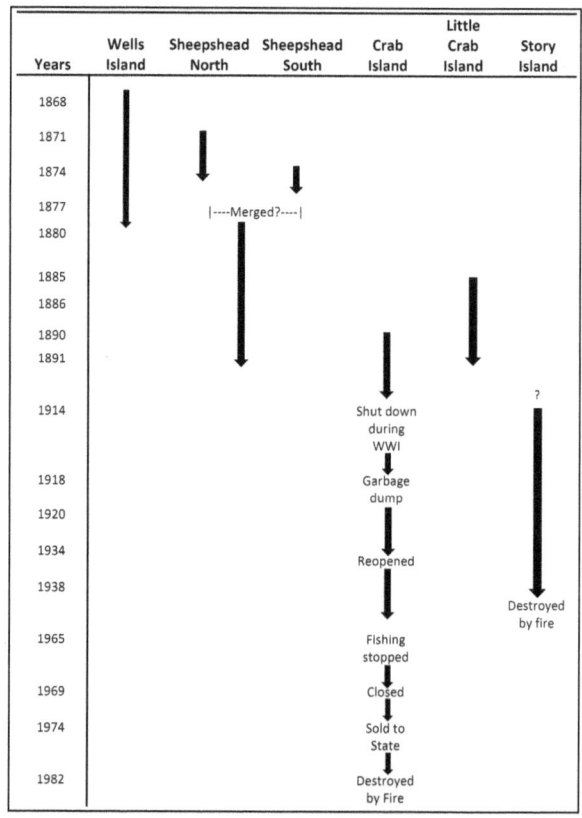

Fig. 3. Period of operations for individual fish factories in the Mullica Valley. *Courtesy Kenneth W. Able.*

Manufacturing from Menhaden

At approximately the same time, another factory opened on Little Crab Island near Shooting Thoroughfare (Fig. 3, 4), but this operation only remained active for a short duration. The only remnants are some pilings at the edge of the marsh (Fig. 5) and a few bricks a local clammer tonged up.[3] During the same time period, when all three factories operated simultaneously, the largest and most enduring factory was established a short distance away on Crab Island. The sixth and most recently constructed factory, sited on Story Island near the earlier factories in the Sheepshead Meadows, dates to circa 1914. This factory suffered a fire circa 1938, but much of its ruins remain intact today (Fig. 6).

The Stinkhouse on Crab Island

The recorded history of the fish factory on Crab Island documents not only the many changes at this fishery, but also the advancement in processing menhaden as well as the overall industry decline. After its establishment in the 1890s (see early photo from 1906, Fig. 7), the fishery operated until World War I, when the U. S. Government seized many of the fishing vessels for the war effort. Crab Island did not reopen immediately after the war, but served as an Atlantic City dump for several years, with the garbage arriving in barges. During hot weather periods, the grease overflowing from the barges created a sheen on the water's surface, making it difficult for clammers to firmly grasp their rakes.[5] Others recall the carcasses of dead horses laying on the docks waiting to be incinerated.[6] Photographs of

Fig. 4. Location of fish factories in the Mullica Valley. *Courtesy Kenneth W. Able.*

artifacts from the dump (e.g. pieces of pottery, rings, etc.) can be found in the files of the Tuckerton Historical Society.

Fig 5. Old dock pilings that indicated the location of the former fish factory at Little Crab Island. *Photograph by Pete Stemmer, August 27, 2010.*

Fig. 6. Remains of the fish factory on Story Island. *Photograph by Pete Stemmer, August 27, 2010.*

Fig. 7. Crab Island fish factory in the Great Bay portion of the Mullica Valley during the early days. *Courtesy of the Tuckerton Historical Society.*

Fig. 8 Crab Island fish factory circa 1960, during its most intense period of operation. *Courtesy of the Tuckerton Historical Society.*

Manufacturing from Menhaden

Fig. 9. Menhaden cookers in the Crab Island factory. *Courtesy of the Tuckerton Historical Society.*

Fig. 10. Menhaden fish meal bag from Crab Island fish factory. *Photograph by K. W. Able from material contributed by Lisa Auermuller.*

Fig. 11. Menhaden fishing boats tied up at the Crab Island fish factory. *Courtesy of the Tuckerton Historical Society.*

The factory began processing menhaden again circa 1934. In the mid-twentieth century, this factory reached its zenith when the buildings on Crab Island resembled and functioned like a small city. The approximately 100-acre island included the fish oil and meal processing facilities (Fig. 8), which were state-of-the-art for the period. After the boats offloaded the menhaden, workmen transported the catch to the steam cookers (Fig. 9) and then the pressers, where pumps sent the expressed liquid (water, oil, blood) to separators, thereby isolating the oil from the other liquids. Following pressing, the fish carcasses underwent drying and were then stored in the scrap shed until a conveyor carried them to a grinding mill, where chutes sent the finished meal into burlap sacks through the bagger (Fig. 10), preparatory for transport to various markets. Workers often took the "good fish," such as weakfish or bluefish, snagged in the seine along with the menhaden, and salted them down, placing them in barrels (later in freezers) for human consumption.

After World War II, the fishery gradually replaced its wooden steam fishing vessels with steel vessels that continued using the large purse seines (Fig. 11). The Coast Guardsmen assigned to Station 119, at the end of the Sheepshead Meadows at Little Egg Inlet, from its construction in 1937 until it was abandoned in 1962, tracked the numerous vessels coming and going from the

Fig. 13. One of the tugboats used to move people, fish meal, and supplies from the Crab Island fish factory to the mainland. *Photograph courtesy of the Tuckerton Historical Society.*

Fig. 12. Steam fishing vessels from the Crab Island fish factory at their winter location at Allen's Dock upstream in the Bass River. *Courtesy of the Tuckerton Historical Society.*

Fig. 14. In 1982, fire destroyed much of the fish factory on Crab Island. This photograph, taken August 27, 2010, shows the remaining structures. *Photograph courtesy of Pete Stemmer.*

Stinkhouse to the ocean and back.[7] The fishing vessels often spent the winter tied up as far away as Salisbury Maryland, Atlantic City, or upstream off the Bass River at Allen's Dock (Fig. 12), which still exists today, after the menhaden had migrated into more southerly waters below Cape Hatteras. In addition to the fishing vessels attached to Crab Island, tugboats (Fig. 13) served there to aid in docking and moving the fishing boats in and transporting people and supplies to and from the mainland and to Atlantic City.

The Crab Island "city" included bunkhouses for the workers, typically a transient population of local and seasonal workers from Atlantic City: southern blacks, schoolboys during the summers, and sometimes whole families that lived in individual shacks on the island. Enough people lived on the island, often as many as 100 and by some accounts up to 200, that the "city" had its own general store, which carried a variety of goods from candy to clothes. The managers often lived in nearby Tuckerton and commuted to the island as needed. The island also had many buildings dedicated to fish processing including a "scrap" shed where bagged meal was stored until transported off island. The city featured its own water tower, constructed in 1947 and extant today, although now it only serves the peregrine falcons or barn owls that nest there. In addition, visiting hunters used two large houses on the island. One of the most prominent features on the Island was a runway for small planes, placed in service after WWII for spotting menhaden schools offshore and directing fishing vessels to them. Remnants of the runway can still be seen in aerial images and detected if you are brave enough to wade through the dense forests of poison ivy that now dominate the island.

The large drying racks on the waterfront, viewed in many old photographs, provide evidence for the large seine nets the fish factory vessels used. The fishery put the racks to good use, making frequent net repairs after shark attacks during deep-sea fishing operations. The refuse released into the Great Bay during the menhaden processing apparently attracted sharks, based on multiple accounts of catching such predators in large numbers. Hook and line fishermen hauled in many of them.

The "city" was largely self-sufficient except for electricity, which power lines carried to the island via Great Bay Boulevard and then extended across the meadows just east and south of Little Sheepshead Creek before passing by submerged cable across Newman's Thoroughfare. The power line supports still exist today, but nesting ospreys usually occupy the tops of the poles, now long devoid of wires.

Parts of the "city" extended across Newman's Thoroughfare and onto the adjacent Seven Bridges Road (now Great Bay Boulevard, bisecting the Sheepshead Meadows). To enhance transferring menhaden products to the mainland and on to market, the fishery company dredged a new channel from Seven Bridges Road, through the salt marsh and Little Sheepshead Creek. At the end of the channel nearest the road, the company dredged a new boat basin and constructed a warehouse. The new channel connected the newly dredged boat basin to Newman's Thoroughfare and Crab Island. Company tugboats pulled barges of bagged fish meal to the warehouse, where waiting trucks received the bagged fish meal, crossed the weigh scales, and then departed to transport the meal to market. The warehouse closed down concomitantly with the Crab Island facility. For a brief period subsequent to its closure, the former fish meal warehouse served as a clam hatchery. Later, the building burned down in a suspicious fire and was then razed. Today, a number of organizations use the site to house scientific meteorological instruments. The boat basin remains, along with remnants of the docks.

In the early 1960s, the facility at Crab Island began processing the menhaden into high-protein fish flour. It continued in operation until fishing for menhaden ceased in 1965 due to economics and the reduced quantity of fish. From 1965 to 1969, the factory processed fish scraps from Louisiana into animal feed. In 1969, the factory finally closed, but a crew of eight individuals lived onsite to maintain the facility in case it reopened. In 1974, the State of New Jersey acquired the land and buildings, along with the rest of the Seven Islands and adjacent Sheepshead Meadows. The state then created the Great Bay Wildlife Management Area from this acquisition. In 1982, a fire destroyed most of the remaining factory buildings, leaving only the structural framing and a water tower as mute sentinels of past activities (Fig. 14).

Despite the numerous facilities dedicated to processing menhaden that once existed along the east coast of the United States (in 1955 there were 23 fish factories), only a single one, in Reedville, Virginia, continues operations today.[8]

Endnotes

Acknowledgements
Numerous individuals assisted in bringing this story together, particularly Pete Stemmer. Other members of the Tuckerton Historical Society provided access to documents and photos that proved central to this study. Paul Hart also provided information from the files of the Tuckerton Seaport. H. Heinrich offered personal anecdotes of his time at Crab Island. Staff at the Rutgers University Marine Field Station, especially Maggie Shaw and Stacy Van Morter, assisted in the gathering of literature and preparation of images. Carol Van Pelt carefully prepared several typescript drafts of this manuscript.

Ken Able is a Distinguished Professor in the Department of Marine and Coastal Sciences and is Director of the Marine Field Station at Rutgers University. His interests are diverse and include the life history and ecology of fishes with emphasis on habitat quality as well as the natural history of the Mullica Valley.

1. Roger W. Harrison, "The Menhaden Industry," *Investigational Report No. 1* (Washington: Government Printing Office, 1931).
2. W. Ross Yates, *Joseph Wharton: Quaker Industrial Pioneer* (Plainsboro: Associated University Press, 1987).
3. Evidence can be found in the Tuckerton Historical Society photo files.
4. Kenneth W. Able, *Station 119: From Lifesaving to Marine Research* (West Creek, NJ: Down the Shore Publishing, 2015).
5. Ibid.
6. Edmunds, Lori. "The Stinkhouse on Crab Island" *Tuckerton Historical Society* (2010), http://tuckertonlehhs.org/stinkhouse-on-crab-island.php.
7. Able, *Station 119*.
8. Susan C. Waters, "Menhaden," *Virginia Marine Resource Bulletin* 26 (1994): 3.

Risley School, Estell Manor, Atlantic County, New Jersey. On November 21, 1906, a young schoolteacher named Ira Ten Boeck Smith sent a post card inscribed with "Some of my youngsters" to Margaret Treen Abbott of Mays Landing, New Jersey. Smith mailed the card at the Risley Post Office, since he taught at the one-room schoolhouse there. In June 1907, Smith received his county certificate for instructing second-grade students; he had just turned 19 years of age the month before. Despite receiving his certification, it appears he only taught during the 1906 – 1907 school year at Risley. The enumerator during the 1910 federal decennial census failed to record an occupation for Ira, but by the following year, he was editor of the *Atlantic County Record*, a weekly newspaper published in Mays Landing. He also served as an Atlantic County Freeholder. He died in August 1957 and the Union Cemetery in Mays Landing received his remains. In February 1980, Ira's daughter, Barbara Smith Irwin, donated five items that had belonged to her father to the New Jersey Historical Society in Newark. The collection includes four photographs of the Risley School and Ira's class book from 1906. This book would likely yield the name of the blind girl in the front row of this post card image.

Carabajal, The Jew

A Legend of Monterey, Mexico

Charles K. Landis

INTRODUCTION

By Vince Farinaccio

"Carabajal, The Jew—A Legend of Monterey, Mexico" was written during the last significant literary phase in the career of Charles K. Landis, founder of Vineland and Sea Isle City and co-founder of Hammonton. Landis's interest in writing fiction can be traced back to the 1840s, when, as an adolescent, he produced a lengthy story set in Egypt. He followed this text, in the early 1850s, with a prelude to the earlier Egyptian tale before setting aside his literary aspirations to launch a law practice in Philadelphia prior to his real estate ventures. Landis soon turned his attention to non-fiction and, over the ensuing four decades, prodigiously recorded his experiences in journals, articles, essays, letters and legal documents, returning to fiction whenever a lull occurred between major projects.

The founding of Vineland in 1861, and its subsequent development into a successful town over the next nine years, precluded Landis from creating any fictional works during this time frame. In the 1870s, he devoted himself to maintaining his journals, producing travelogues, and writing editorial-like essays defending or exhorting various causes. After his acquittal, however, in the fatal shooting of Uri Carruth, the editor of the weekly newspaper *The Vineland Independent* who relentlessly harangued Landis with incessant articles and editorials denouncing him as a fraud, an opportunist, and a detriment to the very settlement he had founded, Landis resumed his fictional pursuits, in 1878, with a science-fiction novel, *A Trip to Mars*. The founding of Sea Isle City and other endeavors during the 1880s forced another hiatus from fiction writing, and he did not return to his literary ambitions until 1894, when he drafted the historical fiction "Carabajal" and the fable "Autobiographical Sketch of a Tree," reminiscent of such works as James Fenimore Cooper's 1843 tale, *Autobiography of a Pocket-Handkerchief*. It is impossible to identify

Charles K. Landis, c. 1861, the year he founded Vineland.
Courtesy of the Vineland Historical & Antiquarian Society.

these works of fiction as derivative of their antecedents since Landis carefully imbued each with his own personal philosophy and concerns.

Reflecting on his texts, virtually all of Landis's writings are suffused with autobiographical elements. He consistently put on display his life and perspectives throughout his non-fiction, but they are present in his fictional works as well. *A Trip to Mars*, for example, contains Landis's socio-economic concerns, his utopian viewpoint, and hints at some of his personal experiences, even employing a group of characters based on acquaintances from his 1874 European trip. His fiction of the early 1890s offers a similar peek into his life.

Landis claims he encountered the story of the late sixteenth-century Portuguese explorer/colonizer Luis de Carabajal y Cueva in Monterey during his first trip to Mexico early in 1894. The extant portion of his journal from this period reveals that he arrived in Monterey on March 22 and remained there until at least March 24, the last date of the surviving entries. During that time, he records no mention that he encountered the tale of Carabajal in written or oral form. Yet, at some point, he managed to learn of the explorer's exploits and turn them into a source of inspiration.

Landis saw his protagonist as a kindred spirit—much as he had seen Pennsylvania founder William Penn and fictional outlier Don Quixote—who shared with the Vinelander an endurance in the face of opposition and a romantic notion that prevailed against adversity. It is easy to discern what drew Landis to Carabajal and compelled him to use the Portuguese adventurer as the focus of his story. The sacrosanct beliefs that guided the explorer and fueled his vision surely appealed to the author. Carabajal's success in establishing his colony, his continued practice of Judaism within a largely Roman Catholic system, and his steadfastness in confronting the judgment of others were admirable facts and reminiscent of Landis's own achievements, resolve and perseverance. The treatment Landis experienced at the hands of individuals like Carruth, and supporters of *The Independent*, was not unlike a political Inquisition targeting anyone who stood in the way of its views.

In shaping his version of Carabajal's tale, Landis embraced the explorer's determination, vision, and accomplishments as a town founder but, as a principled individual, he stopped short of acknowledging the vices that offended his own morality. He carefully skirted Carabajal's indulgence in slave trading in Northern Africa and in New Spain, where the explorer actively engaged in capturing and selling Indians for profit — actions that contributed in part to his eventual arrest and incarceration. The variations Landis applies to Carabajal's life are more of a sly wink to the reader rather than a blatant disregard for the facts, and there is no better evidence of this than when he provides his protagonist with a checklist he deemed necessary in establishing a worthy settlement, a list that is more than a bit familiar to Landis's own development activities.

Carabajal's Nuevo Leon settlement, according to Landis's rendering of the legacy, succeeded due to the design upon which he had built the colony. He cites "agricultural and manufacturing development," "the educational and the aesthetic," the establishment of "free libraries," and "wide streets, wide enough for decoration and a double row of shade trees" to attract "birds which are essential in the cultivation of fruits by destroying insect enemies." Houses, we are told, should be "set a certain distance back from the roadside in order to afford room for flowers and shrubbery." It is stipulated that the founder should provide access to markets for the sale of agricultural and manufactured products, and "see that the inexperienced colonists should not fall into the hands of dishonest consignors or commission men, and in this way be robbed of their toil."

The checklist of Nuevo Leon's design is the same one Landis used in the founding of Vineland, which he had similarly developed as an agricultural and manufacturing community. The precise plan Landis employed required that homes be set back at least twenty-five feet to provide planting space for flowers and shrubbery. Shade trees lined the streets, offering, as Landis pointed out, safe harbor for birds, which rid the town of insects harmful to the fruit grown in his settlement. One-hundred-foot-wide avenues became the primary roads. The arts, along with social awareness and progressive thinking, were promoted through lectures and performances at Plum Street Hall. Landis sought to establish an exemplary education system, a free library and diverse industrial offerings. A train station at the center of the town connected businesses to markets in Philadelphia and New York, and efforts were made to establish a public market in Vineland. Landis also maintained vigilance over the workers of his town and, three years prior to writing "Carabajal," dispatched a law to the governor of New Jersey that would protect farmers and fruit growers from being defrauded by those he considered commission men. For his efforts, he was branded a dangerous individual, much like the protagonist of his historical fiction.

What prevents "Carabajal" from being reduced to a mere marketing ploy for Vineland and its success stems from Landis's ability to tell a good story, a talent he had exhibited from his earliest literary attempts. His talent proved particularly effective in rendering action sequences, a skill that can best be witnessed in *A Trip to Mars*, which contains an extended adventure that is rather riveting in its execution. "Carabajal" incorporates similar moments just as measured and captivating as those in the earlier novel.

While "Carabajal" may contain autobiographical elements, Landis's life isn't the only one woven through the threads of his narrative. Until the 1890s, there had been a reluctance to address his family's history in his own writings, but in 1888 he had received word that a Pennsylvania relative, David B. Landis, had been researching and compiling a book about their family's ancestry, including the death of the Swiss Mennonite martyr Hans Landis in 1614. Hans Landis died as a result of the Inquisition, and the continued persecution of his kin prompted their migration to America. Landis undoubtedly read the book when published and he probably recognized in the tale of Carabajal an opportunity to reflect the story of his ancestor, whose death followed Carabajal's by only several decades. His family's succeeding plight resulted from the same controlling force that tormented the Portuguese explorer's relatives. For the only time in his writing career, Landis chose to acknowledge his family's history, but only by disguising it in the context of the tale about another man whose fate bore a remarkable resemblance.

The fact that "Carabajal" was the only literary work by Landis published during his lifetime should not be overlooked. It appears he discovered, in the final decade of his life, a way to allegorically tell his own tale and that of his ancestors. Along with the towns he created and the many accomplishments he accrued, the story contributes to what can be considered an esteemed legacy. The fact that "Carabajal" is now available again for a new generation of readers is a testament to that legacy.

Carabajal, The Jew

A Legend of Monterey, Mexico

(Copyrighted September 18th, 1894)

Monterey is one of the loveliest places in Mexico. It is upon a small plain, surrounded by the most picturesque of mountains. Its plazas, streets, and architecture remind one of some of the cities of southern Italy. As we walk through this beautiful old city, and look out upon its mountains, surrounding it upon all sides, we cannot but feel an interest in the place. It existed when Boston, New York and Philadelphia were not thought of, and when we think of how far a way from civilization it was three hundred years ago, how completely isolated, we wonder who could have been the consummate and daring genius who established it, and made it possible in that age. When we come to look back through the vista of years, we discover one of the most interesting and darkest events of history, full of heroism, confidence, perfidy, and meanness of humankind. We will begin:

Philip II of Spain was in his small private cabinet in the palace of the Escurial. It looked like the office of a man, partly business like and partly literary in his pursuits, but not the office of a king. Philip did an immense amount of Cabinet work—too much of it for the good of his Kingdom. Had he been out in the world more, and sometimes at the head of his armies, like his energetic father Charles V, it might have been better for Spain. Nearby stood his minister of Finance. Strange as it may appear, the subject of dire perplexity, was the want of money. This Emperor of a large part of Europe and of the Indies, in the latter part of his reign was one of the poorest men in his Kingdom, if poverty can be reckoned in proportion to his wants.

At length he said, "I have it."

The minister looked surprised.

"I have been greatly pained" said the king, "to have heard such direful reports from the Province of Santa Lucia in Mexico, of the massacres by these savage tribes of Indians. There is a man whom I have in mind, capable of checking all this, and making that Province an example of prosperity. He has enterprise, skill and bravery, and large creative talent, and a vast amount of wealth."

"Who may this be?" asked the minister.

"Don Louis de Carabajal Y Cueva" answered the King.

"He is a Jew," said the minister.

"All the better," replied the King "for this reason, he will expect less and pay more. My scheme is, to offer him the Governorship of this new Kingdom of New Leon, and to request at the same time a loan of two millions. This cures the evils of that distracted country and enables me to partly pay the army, and make the expedition to Africa."

"But Carabajal will also want soldiers," said the minister.

"Never mind," replied the King, "Carabajal's fertility of resource is such, that he will do all things, without costing me a cent. Besides this, Carabajal is a humanitarian, and I can trust him with my people."

The minister's prejudices were intense, and narrow, but he knew that it was not best to argue with a king, and especially King Philip.

Carabajal, true, he was a Jew, and true, as Philip said, he was a humanitarian. Christ, by nationality, was a Jew, and how much of an atheist any one may be, or how much of an unbeliever, all will admit, that he himself, was a humanitarian, though his pretended followers have deluged the world with blood. Carabajal was born in the village of Magodorio, in the Kingdom of Portugal, in the year 1539. He was the son of a Hebrew, who had acquired vast wealth, how, history does not inform us. It is rumored that his mother was from Greece or Asia. His father was a peculiar man, and had few or no personal intimates, consequently, at this distance of time, almost nothing is known of his history. He educated his son by private tutors. The son was a good student, and a reader; this education in some degree accounts for his lack of the knowledge of human nature, at least the evil that is in it, and his unreserved confidence, the noblest and most unfortunate of qualities. His education and extensive reading and travel, improved, elevated, and liberalized his mind. In due time he married a woman of his own race with all the noble and womanly qualities, which belong so intrinsically to the Jews; which have blessed that race, with the most faithful of mothers, the truest of conjugal love, and the happiest of homes. Let us look around the world, and where do we find a more domestic people than the Jews, and this blessing they owe most largely to that womanhood, which their God has given them, to console them in their many afflictions.

Combined with a love of Art and of Music, so often characteristic of this people, Carabajal, without possessing shrewdness or cunning, had all the business sagacity of his race. Whether he invested his money in Portugal, Spain or Turkey, it appeared to double itself in a little time, in short, what he touched turned into gold. His genius, and taste in Art, and his public spirit induced him to find many of the lost treasures of past ages, in literature, and art, with which he enriched the universities and art galleries of Spain, in order that they might confer the greatest possible benefit, in the shortest possible time. He also established many institutions of Charity, such as hospitals, homes for foundlings, erring women, old people, and orphans. The benefit of these institutions was not selfishly confined to his own race, but was open to all mankind. This great mind, was like the sun of God, too elevated to be controlled by the petty prejudices, and sectarianism of man, shedding its blessed rays upon all alike. Noticing the large number of his countrymen, who were sorely oppressed, and poverty-stricken in Portugal and Spain, besides other people, some years before, he purchased a large territory in the then Province of Penuco, near Tampico, Mexico, and established there, what the Spaniards call, a hacienda, practically a new colony. Here he decided to try a philanthropic experiment, not in the way of charity, but that of helping people to help themselves, and to encourage his own people, in a life of agriculture and stock-raising, knowing that the first essential to making them farmers, was to make terms with them, by which they would come into the absolute, or what is known in English law, the fee simple, of the land. There were no gold seeking inducements held out, consequently, the people who were attracted by this scheme, were an entirely different class from those who would have been attracted by the prospects of finding gold mines, and of subduing Indians, to work them as slaves. His ideas of a colony were not vague, but were reduced to certain principles, founded upon the great Laws governing human nature. The first principle was industry, as he knew that this was not only essential, to worldly success or prosperity, but happiness. It was his custom to write his plans and ideas upon all subjects, in this way he found them more definitely formed or designed in his mind. In doing this he has left some thoughts which were truly philosophical and do him the highest honor. (See Appendix.)

As said before, Carabajal bought a large track [sic] of land, and fully carried out these ideas. He also extended the hand of fellowship to the Indians, in the neighborhood and found them not only coadjutors, but teachers in his work. They taught the Hebrew colonists, how to make their beautiful pottery, and also hand-woven stuffs, not only how to make them, but instructed them in their decorative arts, which were far superior to anything they expected to find and well worthy of imitation. They also instructed them in growing many things well adapted to the climate, and new to Europeans. No slavery was allowed in the colony. The result was that the country was filled with industry and peace, and music was heard in every house. Under this benign influence, the colony increased and prospered, and ship loads of produce were sent to Spain, to return well-laden with more of the oppressed Jews of Europe. With these ship loads of produce, he always sent a watchful agent, to see that it brought full market prices, and that his farmers were consequently not cheated out of their wealth. It would be an enchanting sight could we only go to the Plaza, in the center of the great Hacienda, some moonlight evening, to see the happy youth of the place enjoying the dance, to the sound of music and song, the old folks quietly looking on. The fame of this successful and prosperous colony soon spread over Spain and Portugal. Heretofore all colonies had been established upon the basis of slave-labor and gold-seeking. This made its success a greater surprise to the sordid materialist and due credit was given Carabajal, for a great deal of shrewdness, cunning and energy. The debased souls of these men never for once conceived that the elements of success had been wisdom, honesty and humanity.

When Carabajal was approached by the minister of Philip, on the subject of the loan, he was at the time in Madrid. He had visited Spain, to look after the interests of his colonists. The proposal was coupled with the offer of the Governorship of the northern part of Mexico, as in part a security for the loan, but to continue to himself, and his heirs, independently of the viceroy of Mexico. He was to be allowed to repay himself if he chose, out of the revenues of which would be coming to the crown, but independently of this, the King of Spain promised to pay him. Carabajal was dazzled, not by the vanity of holding such a position, but by the prospects of the infinite amount of good he might be enabled to do. The territory was to be called the Kingdom of New Leon, and embraced a tract of 200 leagues square, including his beloved colony of Penuco, and also Tampico. It included the states of Tamaulepas, Nuevo Leon, Coshuila, Parts of San Luis, Tacatecas Durango, Chihuahua and Texas. Establishing this territory into a new kingdom was a reasonable assurance that all was meant in good faith, but alas, Carabajal should have considered that there could be no assurance against the state, that the instant State Policy should change, that the moment he became Governor under Philip, he lost his liberty, and the utter variance, religiously and morally, between himself and the powers and the people of Spain. But instead of this, it appeared to him, that he would have more power and upon a larger theatre, where he could benefit humanity, in the largest possible degree, not only the people he would take to the new world, but the native inhabitants, the same as he had done at Penuco. Montemayer, his private Secretary, was also carried away and dazzled by the brilliant baits held out by Philip. This Secretary, Carabajal loved as a dear son. His parents had died early, and he had taken the orphan boy, and educated him, as his own, and finally made him his private Secretary.

It was not long before the negotiations were closed. Philip obtained his money, and Carabajal received his "Royal Patent" as Governor of the new Kingdom of Leon, which as said before was to be hereditary in his own family.

I may here state, that a few years before this, an attempt had been made by some Spaniards, and

Tlaxcalan Indians, to found a settlement upon the stream of Santa Lucia in Monterey, which settlement they called Santa Lucia, but the Indians of the North came down in force and almost exterminated them, and drove them away.

The rumor of this new grant and enterprise was soon spread over Spain and Portugal, and much of Europe, and an army of adventurers offered themselves, all anxious to enslave Indians, and have them dig gold and silver for them, whilst they should hunt among the mountains, or live in their palaces with numerous concubines, of Indian women. Carabajal did his best to select the best material that presented itself, or that he could find, but this was necessarily influenced, by his position. Now, being a Royal Governor, he could not conventionally, and with decency, refuse some of the poor nobility of Spain, nor the sons of some of the wealthy nobility. Under the orders and instructions, of the Government he could not refuse, also a large contingent of Holy Friars, whose ostensible duty was to convert the Indians, and also to assist Carabajal in many ways, especially in conducting schools, and providing religious consolation and instruction to the colonists.

In due time a fleet was procured, and Carabajal set sail with a large force of men, colonists, arms and supplies, for Tampico. Thence he proposed to march to Penuco, where he would gather up many more colonists, and thence march to Santa Lucia, or what is now known as Monterey, and make it the capital of his Kingdom. He also took with him his family, and many more Jewish emigrants, who he felt could assist his work, by their intelligence and fidelity. The voyage was prosperous, only favoring winds filled their sails. In the progress of it they met a number of whales and schools of porpoises. These things they considered good omens. I do not give the patient reader an account of the vessels, and their numbers, and names of the different cavaliers, as these particulars have not come down to us.

This voyage is supposed to have occurred in 1579 in the fall of the year. A safe landing was made in the beautiful harbor of Tampico, after which the march begun, by way of Penuco. It was made by easy stages, and no difficulties were encountered, because every arrangement had been made for it by the foresight of Carabajal. The whole body was under strict martial law, and the position of every camp in the night was well chosen and guarded. On this march the Spanish cavaliers had much cause for surprise at the military knowledge shown by Carabajal; they naturally supposed that he must have been an experienced soldier, which he was not, and it raised him more in their estimation, than all the virtues he possessed. When they got to Penuco, they were all charmed with its loveliness, its prosperity, its sweet pretty homes embowered in trees and vines. The smiles on the faces of the people, especially the women and children, and all over, that if Carabajal could bring all this about by his own unaided efforts, what might he not do when backed by the authority of the Government.

They tarried here a few days, for rest and refreshments, and then pushed along upon their march until, upon a beautiful fall day they reached the Spring of Santa Lucia. They bathed and refreshed themselves in its sweet translucent waters. Ruin spread around. The buildings of former occupants bore evidence of fire and conflict, destroyed by the savage Apache and Yako Indians, who had been in the habit of pouring down, from the far North, like a storm. There was now plenty of work to do, and the sympathy arising from a common danger, produced peace and harmony among Indians and Spaniards. What a blessed thing is labor. It is a balsam to thought, and to the body, the promoter of appetite, sleep and health and of peace. There was a wholesome sprinkling of the inhabitants of Penuco amongst them.

Carabajal laid the grounds out with a reference to beauty, convenience and health. He adopted Jewish sanitary regulations, and a special Board for carrying them out. No cess pools were allowed to be dug in the soil. The closet box, shovel, and dry earth were used, which at certain periods were emptied and used as manure, or carried away. The streets were made wide, and the colonists were required to plant trees for shade and health, the same as at Penuco, and the houses required to be placed a certain distance back from the roadside. In those days there was an abundance of timber for building. The country was covered with wood, far up toward the tops of the mountains, and consequently there was an abundant and refreshing rainfall. Martial law was strictly observed, until buildings were erected for homes, and works of defence were made. The Spaniard of the upper class, or cavaliers, spent their time hunting in the mountains, and supplied the camp with bears, deers, wild turkeys and other game; consequently they were fully as useful at that time as any other of the people. Soon as possible, the Holy Fathers started a church, a Monastery, and a Convent. Carabajal did not approve of the two latter, but representing a Roman Catholic Government, he could make no hindrance. He supplemented them by building a small Synagogue for his own people. He did not encourage the locating of many farms at first, as he knew there would have to be a battle with the Northern savages before long; consequently the colony was governed by martial law, for a time, and all the men were drilled and practiced daily in the use of arms. Arquebusses and light cannon were brought from Spain, which, though small, would make a great noise upon their discharge, that would reverberate, and thunder with many echoes, among the surrounding hills.

He appointed a council of five, who under his patent had no real authority, but for purposes of consultation and advice. He at once organized the following societies: Agricultural, Horticultural, Arbor, Literary with Library, Musical and Scientific. He wrote treatises upon the duties and objects of these different societies, and papers upon various subjects, appertaining to these objects, in reference to the country they were in, and its surroundings. There was also deep policy about this move. It distributed a great many offices, satisfied the "amour propre" of a great many people, and at their leisure moments gave them something to do.

He had always been a student of history and of military books. It was his habit to read Caesar's Commentaries once a year, but when he got to this new world, he saw that he would have to adopt an entirely new system of war, from that of Europe. This was his system: First, to always fight under protection, behind trees, rocks or earth-works, never in the open. Second, to have a corps of cavalry whose instructions were never to fight except at an advantage. The rule of its discipline was not to fight, but to hang in the rear and flanks of an enemy, breaking up its communications, and killing all stragglers and foragers. When attacked, to fly and decoy the enemy into ambushes, or to return immediately to the same tactics when the pursuit was over. In this way the murdering and burning, resulting from Indian raids were stopped, as they would naturally be kept together, and also made timid by being mystified, as to the number they had to oppose.

The fame of this settlement brought many friendly Indians to it, but nevertheless a doubt hovered over it, on account of the anticipated attack of the terrible Yakos, and until it was found as to how they would be resisted. However, in the presence of danger and with plenty to do, there was universal harmony, and obedience to the Governor. He had sent about a dozen friendly Indians to the far North, as spies with instructions, for some always to remain there, and use the others as couriers, to give him information, and always, for safety, to send at least three couriers by different trails, in case some of them should be killed upon the way.

One particularly beautiful day, when everything appeared as calm and quiet as Heaven itself, one of these couriers was seen coming in all haste, over a hill by trail, from the North. When Carabajal's attention was called to him, he went out to meet him, but before he could give any information, and before he reached him, he fell down dead with fatigue. Carabajal knew what it meant. A signal gun was fired, which signified that all should return from the hunt, and an immediate muster. Within an hour or two another courier appeared, and he gave information that a Yako army of a thousand mounted warriors, were on their way to attack them.

The Yakos and Apaches were Indians that had never been conquered. Large and strong of build, fierce of disposition, they inhabited mountain fastnesses in the far North where it was impossible to pursue them. They were a different race from the Aztecs, the Pueblos and the peaceable, civilized and industrious Indians of Mexico, who lived by agricultural pursuits. Their plan was to attack by superior numbers, and by sudden surprise. They spared neither the old, the women nor children, they made a barrier against the settlement of the north of Mexico, and the working of its fertile valleys and rich silver mines. The tactics of the Spaniards had been heretofore unable to cope with them. They now had a different man to meet.

Carabajal had made several expeditions to the North, with the sole object of studying the topography of the country and a view to military encampments and positions. By the next morning his little army was on its march. Heretofore it had been customary to await the attack of the savages, and it was with much doubt and fear that the friendly Indians remaining in the camp saw them file away over the mountains, the sun brightly glancing upon spear and helmet. But Carabajal and his little band had full confidence. They believed in the system of their fighting and strategy as much as the soldiers under Hannibal believed in theirs when they went to meet the heretofore unconquerable Romans in their own country.

After two days' march a halt was made upon the trail behind a collection of high rocks, in different masses, and which lined the trail on both sides. The cavalry, which was instructed not to fight, was sent forward to continue the march north. They had not gone far before they saw the van of these redoubtable warriors, splendidly mounted. The Yakos were much astonished to meet with an armed force so far away from Santa Lucia, and halted to await, prepared to throw out wings to surround the foe during his attack, which was their usual strategy.

What was their surprise when they found that the foe did not attack. They sent out a few horsemen, who reported that the Spaniards were behind a hill in inferior force, and that fully twenty of them fled, when the Yakos numbered only ten. This whetted the appetite of the Indians. They determined to make a feint of attack to see what the Spaniards would do. What was their surprise when they saw the Spaniards flee. These brave soldiers, whose pride it had heretofore been to stand and fight and die! They made up their minds they would be an easy prey; that all they had to do was to pursue and conquer. This they did pell mell. It appeared to be their only wish on earth to catch this little band of three hundred horsemen.

But the three hundred were well mounted and could well lead the pursuit. The Yakos appeared to be gaining ground, and had bright hopes of reaching them, until all of a sudden every rock along the trail for a mile appeared to be a volcano of fire, death and thunder. Down the riders went. Suddenly the trail was closed, and over a mighty rock upon it thundered artillery with cannon balls and grape shot. They turned to flee, but the route from which they came was also closed. Now there appeared to be unseen death upon every side. Whilst they were being killed with bullets, arrows and cannon balls, they could see no foe to fight, until as they attempted to flee, foes on foot and horse, appeared to be everywhere, whilst the terrible arquebusses and artillery pursued them, with certain death. Their destruction was a matter of but a few minutes, though it appeared to be hours; no mercy was shown them and none was asked, but none escaped except a very few, who hid themselves among the rocks. Carabajal thought that true mercy would be in giving them a bloody lesson, and he was right.

When his little army marched back to Santa Lucia, they brought several hundred good horses, a quantity of good and beautiful serapis or blankets captured from their foes, and other evidences of victory. As for baggage there was none to capture; these warriors travelled and fought upon a package of Tortillas, a little bag of parched corn, and what meat or game they might pick up on their way. When they entered the little town every body was wild with delight at the idea that those heretofore victorious warriors had been so completely defeated. The victory gave Carabajal unbounded influence among all his colonists, and enabled him to at once start upon his plans for carrying on his colony, but he knew that the storm would gather again. These Indians would look upon their defeat as a pure accident of war, and would soon be coming down with twice their previous force, and that before long, but he had confidence in the excellent spies, who almost the day after the battle, were sent North. Of all that band of invaders, only two or three were left alive, and returned to their country, to carry the news. It spread terrible lamentations throughout the Indian land, but of that kind that calls for revenge, instead of dispair. The war dances immediately commenced, and they sent couriers with arrows North, to the terrible Apaches to join them in the invasion.

In the meantime Carabajal had laid his city out, on a most beautiful plan, wide streets, wide enough for decoration and a double row of shade trees with spaces in the intersections, for fountains and statuary, where animals and men could water, and the latter also drink in beauty and instruction with their eyes. In all the deeds given he provided that these trees should not only be planted, but never removed, the same about the fountains and statues, also that all the houses should be set a certain distance back from the roadside in order to afford room for flowers and shrubbery, and that convenient seats should be placed along the streets and roads for the rest and comfort of pedestrians, and what was of as much importance, that the grade or levels should not be changed, thus affording no opportunity to future city councils to make jobs, by which the people might be conveniently robbed, and their shade trees destroyed, under the specious pretext of improving the grade of the streets as has been so often done in later times and especially in our own United States.

He also made allotments to the Indians, who wished to farm, and also contracted to give them deeds, by the payment of small sums when the land was paid for. This was a novelty, as most all lands had heretofore been only rented, but Carabajal knew that to give the Indians an absolute ownership in the land they cultivated, thus securing their homes, was the one way to make them permanent and patriotic subjects. At the same time he allotted the mines, in the mountains near by, but under no consideration would he allow the Indians to he enslaved. They worked upon a sort of co-operative wage plan, which even to this day is in vogue in some parts of Mexico. At first the Spaniards were so much opposed to this that an open rebellion was threatened, but at a private meeting held for the purpose Carabajal explained that under this plan they would mine more silver and get more silver and have less risk and responsibility. Fortunately he was supported in his argument by one of the good Catholic Fathers, and persuaded them to make the experiment, which, to their surprise, worked with the greatest degree of success, but none of them wanted to farm. A pastoral home, conjugal and paternal love, were nothing in their minds in comparison to the dross of hard silver and gold, which did them no good when they got it. Such is the madness of man.

He also paid attention to manufactures. He decided to encourage those kinds that were native to Mexico, and they were numerous. He sent to Puebla and brought down the Navajoe Indians to teach the manufacture of serapis (the blankets which are worn over the shoulders). He sent to Guadalajara for potters and had taught the making of the beautiful Indian Pottery of that section, which for artistic beauty and variety is unexcelled of its kind, also the weaving of mats for tables and floors out of cotton in varied figures and colors. He had done all this before at Penuco. He knew how to dispose of these things in Spain, by sending them in his ships from Tampico, which would return with the rich products of Spain, in payment for them, so that by this policy of reciprocity, both countries were benefited and the industry and wealth of the new colonies of Carabajal and which he planted in various parts of the large territories of the new Kingdom of Leon, as it was called, grew immensely.

He knew also that the education the youth of both sexes acquire, has much to do with the happiness of people, of homes, of society and the power and prosperity of a nation. He therefore decided that all education, should in the first place be industrial. He recognized industry, having something to do, as the most important factor in getting the most of happiness and of health out of life. His first consideration was by education also to improve the home life, and he encouraged all children as far as possible to become proficient in the business of their fathers, whether commercial, agricultural, artistic, or manufacturing, in order to bind more closely the home ties to keep families together, and prevent the disposition that otherwise children will have, to go away from home and leave their parents in their old age, when they most need their care and affection. Good agricultural schools were established, connected with farms, gardens, and orchards, to be worked by the pupils, boys and girls. All the arts of preserving were taught in these places. Also industrial schools for teaching textile, mechanical and art work with hand labor, also the theoretical, or scientific part, which was more thoroughly understood and never forgotten when the pupils learned to make practical application of the sciences. The time given to each was about equally divided. The boys were also taught manly exercises, riding horse-back, leaping on and off, the use of the arquebusses, and of artillery, both in slow and rapid movement, in running and leaping, all ending in a military dance, somewhat similar to the Greek Pyrrhic dance. Saturday and Sunday afternoons were especially set apart for these exercises, and it was wonderful to behold the grace and proficiency with which the youth performed them. In all of this music, especially the martial, was not neglected. All of these things appeared to be natural to the Spanish and Indian characters, and are so to this day. Verily, it is a nation now capable of being among the greatest in the world.

It must not be thought that all these things were plain sailing and done without opposition to Carabajal. The good fathers shook their heads, and said that in this education it was the world that was favored, whilst Heaven was forgotten, and to counteract the evil effects they had schools of their own for those they termed "the better classes," where nothing of the industrial was taught, but much of the old classical, the graduates of which seminaries were destined in time to show the effects of their schooling. Whatever envy or jealousy that might exist at that time did not dare show itself. Carabajal was too powerful, and too necessary to them. It was well known that he had loaned an enormous sum to the King, and that he had much more wealth in Spain. His patent of Governorship practically gave him absolute power, almost or quite that of a viceroy, and then his talent was known to be so great in the way of establishing colonies, and in war, that no one felt at that time that he could possibly be dispensed with—the work was new. The colonizatian [*sic*] before had been a failure, and everyone thought that it was Carabajal's mission to make it a success.

Within the next few months, after the last expedition to meet the Indians, besides the work recounted in the foregoing pages, there was also a marked increase of population. Many civilized Indians from Western and Southern Mexico had immigrated to this wonderful colony, which was on the bounding road to rapid improvement, and where the Indian was considered the political equal of the white man, and where justice was meted out to all alike. Numerous vessel loads of immigrants had also arrived from Europe, both Jews and Christians, and even some of the persecuted Moors, who had been driven to Africa, now seeking this glorious Asylum of the West.

When everything was peaceful, full of sunshine and prosperity, another courier arrived from the North with the terrible news that two armies of Indians were about advancing, one army of the Yakos, and another of the Apaches. Their plan was, for the convenience of forage, to march by different trails, one by the Western, the other by the Eastern, and to unite within four days march North of St. Lucia, in order to fall upon it in superior numbers.

Carabajal had made a defence, or citadel, on the top of one of the mountains which surrounds Santa Lucia (Monterey) where there was a large spring of good water, but which mountain it was we are not certain about, but tradition has it that it was the Saddleback. These works were all well provisioned, and here he marched the entire colony that did not go to the war. In this natural citadel they could not be surprised, and could defend themselves against any force that could be brought against them. For the rest he decided to march immediately and strike the enemy with his whole force, in detail, before they had time to join each other. Owing to the fact of not having met them before, he made up his mind to attack the Apaches first, thinking that perhaps he could play the same arts upon them that he had played upon the Yakos. He marched out the next morning early, having sent his skirmishing or decoy cavalry in advance. His artillery consisted of light falconets, that could be carried about anywhere, and were in this way very effective.

It was a question whether he could strike the Apaches before they joined forces with the Yakos or not. They carried very little baggage or impediments, depending upon a good stock of Tortillas, the lightest and most nourishing food in the world for transportation. In a few days they reached the valley among the mountains, where the junction was to take place, and by the blessing of God, there was no Indian sign. This raised the hopes of the little army. In camping no fires were lighted, no noises were allowed. The next day Carabajal decided to select a place for the battle, and await the foe. This was no difficult matter, as the trail ran through a rocky, broken country, consisting largely of mountains and gorges. He selected a spot made, as it were, for concealment, and where also there was a sharp turn in the trail, after running for some distance in a straight line. It was at this turn, concealed by rock and brush, he planted his artillery. Whilst all along on each side for a considerable distance, his men were ranged and entirely concealed. He had not long to wait. They had not much more than made their dispositions, before the thundering tramp of many horses were heard in the distance, and soon appeared his own flying cavalry, apparently in full retreat, but it really was the old manoevre.

They were allowed to pass the angle of the trail, and almost at their heels, came the exultant Apaches, wild with the excitement of apparent victory. They were allowed to come along unmolested, until they were immediately opposite the angle, when artillery belched forth its fire, and the balls ploughed through the ranks of riders, whilst at the same time, from the side of the trail. For nearly a mile poured the fire of the arquebusses or muskets. Down went the riders. On one side of the trail was a steep declivity of several hundred feet, and many horses with their riders, jumped down this place, in pure panic fright. Since the last battle the men of Carabajal had been additionally armed with Javelins and Spanish swords, and they found these weapons terribly effective. The long spears and battle axes of the Apaches availed them but little, against an unseen foe, whilst their ranks were being ploughed with artillery and musketry. It was not long before these warriors were killed or engulfed in the precipice below. The defeat was absolute. A few in the rear turned their horses' heads to the North and escaped, but very few.

The officer commanding the flying cavalry, stated that a few hours before, he came upon their scouts and then their full force, when his whole body turned in apparent flight. When the Apaches saw the flags and banners of the Spaniards, and a large cavalry force, turn and fly, they evidently imagined that it was the Spanish army that had turned in flight, and which they were pursuing. The Spaniards rapidly gathered up their few spoils, of blankets and horses that were worth gathering, and retraced their steps, to gain the point of junction in advance of the Yakos, or to take them by surprise. This was fatiguing after a battle, if battle it could be called. It was an easy march, unencumbered as they were, with baggage or wagons. They decided to make no halt until they reached the spot. In the dusk of the evening, one of their cavalry returned with the information that the Yakos had reached the point of junction and were camping there to await the arrival of the Apaches, of whose disaster they had not heard.

Carabajal resolved to stop where he was, give his men three hours rest and then make a night attack. At this place was a good spring of water, and a level piece of ground. That night was a full moon, the wheels of the artillery were muffled. No fires were kindled. Tortillas and beans were the food of men and horses with full and copious draughts of mountain spring water. He also had prepared with wet gunpowder and dried pine leaves, some barrels of material of which to make a great light, at the time of the attack, on different parts of the field. At the expiration of the three hours, the march was slowly and silently resumed in the night, with the cavalry moving slowly and silently in advance. No talking was allowed, the great danger was from the neighing of horses. On this account the cavalry was ordered to take the rear. About three o'clock in the morning from an acclivity in the trail, they saw the fires, or the embers of fires of the enemy, covering a great space, whilst they were wrapped in the security of profound slumber, the sleep of fatigue, in the open air. The great point was to get as near as possible to them before opening the fires of the attack. The horses of the enemy were pinioned to the ground near each sleeping warrior, who rested upon his arms.

Shortly the army filed to the front in as long a line as practicable, when suddenly the artillery and musketry opened fire and the combustibles prepared to light the field, were set in a blaze with their red and lurid light. The surprise was complete. A part of the command was ordered to charge upon them, and they plied their Spanish swords with fearful effect, whilst the reserve kept up a continuous fire of artillery or falconets and arquebusses, but over the heads of the combatants in fear of killing their own men. The poor Yakos imagined they were attacked by devils, so sudden and unexpected was the onset, the roar of cannon and musketry, the glare of the weird and lurid light, and the stabbing to death by the Spanish swords. Some had the presence of mind to ride away, but most of them were killed, before they could recover their senses. The light of the morning dawn made it all the worse for them, but ended the slaughter. Carabajal sent a force of cavalry after the flying stragglers, and with the rest of his army, after securing the horses and spoils, he marched home. Great was the delight, when from the mountain height, his little army was beheld returning, victorious from two fields. After this brilliant strategy, worthy of Hannibal himself, some of the cavalry who chased the flying Yakos up the trail and over the battle field of the previous day, reported afterwards that thousands of vultures and buzzards were busy at their hedious [sic] feast, and in this way, the few flying Yakos learned the fate of their allies.

Now came years of peace, which gave a fair opportunity to Carabajal to exert its arts. Besides the beautiful Santa Lucia he established some nineteen cities, in different parts of the Kingdom, and farther North where were some of the richest mines. To those cities he gave personal attention, that they might all be well located and laid out, with reference to health, beauty and convenience. Santa Lucia and Penuco were the standards of example. There was no slavery. The same co-operative plan for the mining pervaded every place and the productions were all the greater for it. The agricultural and manufacturing industries worked harmoniously as music, and on all sides sprang up beautiful homes, with vines, figs, the orange, and other fruit trees in the gardens. The streets and roads were lined with trees for shade, under which were placed comfortable benches for rest. Fountains for beauty and for watering stock, and drinking purposes, were placed at the roadsides or intersections of streets and roads, and consequently around the houses, and through the streets, the trees and air were musical with the song of birds. Music and dancing being both natural and part of the education of the people, had the most beautiful and poetic results. At the end of the day, in front of the houses, or in the Alemedas and Plazas, it was as natural for the youth to dance to the sound of the guitar or mandolin, and sing, as it was for them to eat or sleep. An old Spaniard writing home from Santa Lucia said, "He believed that he had fallen into paradise or upon a veritable Arcadia, all was peace, every home, street, and road was beautiful. The people were universally gentle and kind, and so fascinated was he with all these things, he feared he could not leave the country, or would never be happy out of it."

The mines under the co-operative system of labor yielded enormously, which inured greatly to the benefit of the Spanish Government. Carabajal both from motives of policy and principle was scrupulously honest. He sent his tribute twice a year, and did not even retain his loan, preferring to wait the King's convenience to pay it, a convenience which never happened. Population had greatly increased both from Spain and different parts of Mexico, until the prosperity of the Kingdom of Nueva Leon was phenomenal [sic]. Occasionally during his administration some of the Northern settlements would be attacked by the Indians, but these attacks were quickly suppressed and punished by Carabajal.

We before mentioned that he had a Secretary by the name of Montemayer. He was the son of a poor woman who kept a Cantina or wine shop in old Spain. During the repairing of an accident to his carriage one day, Carabajal was so struck with the intelligence, politeness, and quickness of the handsome boy to assist him in repairing his carriage, that he immediately took him into his service. This boy possessed clerical talent, naturally, and he was remarkably executive, when told what to do, but his mind did not reach beyond this. In principle he was thoroughly dishonest, selfish and deceitful. He wore a perpetual smile, talked with a smile, and had the most gentle and winning ways, which had won Carabajal to him, and won every body else that came near him. He had the absolute confidence of Carabajal, and owing to his artfulness and assumption, received credit for much of the success of the policy, and the art and genius which belonged exclusively to his great master. Such is the lack of intelligence in public opinion, that this can easily be. Much like the poor Indian, who, when he saw a man writing words upon paper, wanted the pen that did it, never thinking once, that it could be thought, or even the hand that guided it.

Carabajal had brought his entire family to Santa Lucia, his mother, two sisters, his wife and two daughters, the latter 20 and 22 years old, respectively, and his son, 24 years old, and several nephews and nieces. The son was a cripple, having when very young, been injured in the spine by the neglect of his nurse, but he had a poetical and beautiful soul; some of the finest ballads and music heard through out Mexico and Spain, were of his composition. He was very gentle and beloved by all who knew him, Carabajal had built for himself a commodious house, near the centre of Santa Lucia; that is, a house of stone surrounding a court yard in the centre, decorated with a fountain, flowers, and statuary. The rooms entering upon the Court yard, in the Spanish style, or rather old Roman style.

Spain was so long under the dominion of Rome, that she became essentially Roman, and the invasion of the Vandals, or any other barbarians could not wipe it out. This family set an example of refinement, generosity, and high-bred hospitality to all others. It belonged to no particular set, but with noble liberality belonged to all sets, in order to do the most good. So time rolled on for many years, and all that Carabajal did, was successful, and fortunate, and whatever he touched, seemed to turn, as it were, to gold. Many readers would naturally suppose, that under these happy circumstances, that he had no enemies and that he was surrounded by hosts of friends, and constantly re-assured by expressions of gratitude. This was true only in part. He was guilty with some, of several unpardonable crimes. He was in advance of his time; he was a Jew, and in that age of bigotry, both of these things were very serious. He was honest, and this was wormwood to the corrupt, he was superior in his genius, and magnanimity, and this was ground for both envy and malice. The new World in that age, by many was looked upon only as a field for plunder, and the gratification of the vilest avarice, at the expense of humanity, justice and every sentiment of right. When the Spaniards went to America, it was to gain wealth, gold, and slaves, not by industry, but by force, battle, and adventure. Carabajal stood in direct opposition to these vile objects.

Gold they could have, but only by industry, and they could have no slaves. They considered themselves right; their ideas were founded upon the old laws of feudality; Carabajal's upon those of an advanced humanity, which were not understood. As before related, with him came, at the request of the King, sundry friars, Holy men, to convert the poor Indian and attend to his spiritual wants. In that age all education was in the hands of the Priests, Carabajal made it secular, and by this he acquired the intense hatred of the Priests, more so, being a Jew, as they ascribed it to this fact, as well as all his other principles, so antagonistic to all who were of what was called the better classes of that age. This dissatisfaction was smothered and kept down in the early years of the colony, when it was poor, and in danger, in short, when Carabajal, was considered necessary. But now it was rich, no thought of danger existed, and the Hidalgos and Priests were firmly convinced that they could rule better, and would all make as good generals as Carabajal, especially now that the Indians were thoroughly subdued, or the clouds of war rolled a way so far to the North as not to be seen.

The civilized Indian population had greatly increased in numbers and as they looked upon them, they considered of how many slaves they (The Hidalgos) had been robbed. True, the mines paid well, but they believed that they would pay much more, if worked by slaves, who had to live upon a handful of maze a day, instead of receiving a share of the product. In short they felt, that they were literally robbed by Carabajal, needy adventurers who were beggars when they came into the Kingdom of Leon, and were now rich, had these thoughts. Poor human nature! They had long hoped for the death of Carabajal by some disease, or in battle, as he recklessly exposed himself, but like all such men, he appeared to have a charmed life. Montemayer was the man they pitched upon to govern in his place; they thought that he knew all his master knew, and besides was a very good Christian, so far as the outward performances and ceremonial would indicate.

Montemayer himself knew all of this, and whilst he was pretending the sweetest friendship to his Master, was quietly and in the most treacherous manner fermenting the trouble. But how to supplant and destroy Carabajal, was a very serious question. His power with the people was great; his ability, energy and decision of character were all a terror to him. What was done, would have to be done, in the darkest way possible. The deceit and treachery would have to be of the most consummate kind. It was finally decided by the Hidalgos and the Holy Fathers to introduce the Inquisition into Leon; this had always been successfully opposed by Carabajal, but now they had sufficient influence with the King to order it. The alternative was to submit or rebel. For this Carabajal had no inclination, and submitted. He had better have rebelled; with his superior military talents he could have conquered all Mexico, and made it an independent Kingdom. For this once the unscrupulousness of a Napoleon, would have been a very good thing to possess; but he was not aware, that it was a plot against himself and that his enemies were playing with loaded dice. Being an honest man he was the more easily deceived.

The worthy fathers had built a large stone building, surrounding an entire square, about the site, where is now located the present Iturbide Hotel. In fact this Hotel building was probably a part of it. Everything was barred from the outer world, and as most of their proceedings and trials were of heretic Spaniards and as they most always came out converted, not much attention was attracted to them.

About the same time contrary to the Laws of Carabajal, and during his absence in the North, a bull fight festival was carried on near one of his more Southern cities. A poor Indian Yako, from the far North was accused of being a spy, without any proof excepting prejudice and suspicion, and he was carried into the bull ring, and his limbs tied to four horses, when they were whipped up and he was torn apart to the savage and frantic joy of many of the beholders.

This was the same punishment awarded to the private Secretary of Philip II, for keeping up a secret correspondence, with William, Prince of Orange. This is all mentioned to show how far the influence and fear of Carabajal had weakened under such prosperity of the people, which in their egotism and ingratitude they were so largely inclined to ascribe to themselves, or the natural order of things.

A more than usually severe Indian War had broken out in the North, which as usual commanded the personal attention of Carabajal, and required a long absence. It was now that the Hidalgos commenced conspiring against him with a positive view to his removal or rather murder. They had always hated him, and whilst smiling to his face, would have gladly plunged a dagger in his heart. Now he was away, and many dark and secret meetings were held. They had been active in undermining him in Spain, and also with the viceroy of Mexico, a man who grieved under the superiority of Carabajal, and the contrast between his own government and that of Nueva Leon. Finally it was decided, that it was through the Court of the Inquisition that they would destroy him, and in this way justify themselves, in Mexico, and throughout Europe. The bloody Inquisition, much to the disgust of good Catholics, had become powerful in its secrecy and fanaticism.

Carabajal returned from the War as usual covered with laurels. He was received by the Hidalgos and Priests, with more honor and graciousness than usual; to such a degree that it went to his very heart, and made him happy, happy for himself, and the sake of his family. His dear family, a consideration so great with the Semitic race, from Abraham to Mary, and the same at this day. The love of family is the very household God of their hearts, and no doubt protects them from many of the low vices, common to other races. One evening when Carabajal was enjoying his repose, after a day of great activity, several Hidalgos who were his friends and under great obligations to him, for many most important favors, in short they may be called dear friends, called at the house, and stated that they and the Holy Fathers had arranged a little banquet, in his honor and desired him to step around to their Casa or Palace. It was only a short distance and this he did without suspicion. He had no sooner got there, and the ponderous doors closed their huge jaws behind him, than he was placed under arrest by the warrant of the President of the Inquisition. This terrible order had its own special corps or company of soldiery as a guard, devoted to its service. He was placed at once without respect into a remote and iron-plated chamber, as though he was the most dangerous and vilest of criminals. This having proved so successful, the same artifice was worked with the rest of the family, and under the falsehood, that they were sent for by Carabajal to join in the banquet. The mother, the wife, the sisters, daughters, and son were all decoyed in to the same place, arrested and all imprisoned in separate cells.

We will now state the plan, that the conspirators or rather assassins had decided upon.

It was simply to get Carabajal and his entire family into the dungeons of the Inquisition and under its forms, condemn and execute them all, before any knowledge of it should reach the public.

They knew that he was too powerful to be arrested openly, and that after he was dead, and the crime committed, they could fulminate a lot of outrageous and false charges, to satisfy the public mind and, oh, that my pen should be compelled to write it, I must say that the men, besides the Holy fathers, in the conspiracy, were his supposed to be friends, friends, who in his mind were beyond suspicion. Did not Romulus meet with his supposed apotheosis in the Senate Chamber, in the midst of his best friends, immediately after his return from a great victory, and was never seen afterwards? They gave it out that he was taken bodily up to Heaven, amongst the Gods. Did not the magnanimous and generous Caesar fall beneath the daggers of thirty of his friends, amongst whom was the dearly beloved Brutus? Suspicion never entered the minds of these men, why should Carabajal suspect? Montemayer, his dearly beloved private Secretary, gave it out that everything was right and that Carabajal and family would soon return to their house, and all believed Montemayer.

Carabajal was overwhelmed with indignation and astonishment. He knew much of the iniquities of the Inquisition, but the thought had never occurred to him that it could or would be made the instrument of his own destruction. Now he apprehended the worst, as he knew that unless their designs were of the most fatal character, they would never have dared to perpetrate this indignity, and that he could have neither chance nor hope unless he could communicate with the outside world. He had no idea that they had arrested his own family, or that they had any object in so doing. He did not reflect that his patent of Governorship was hereditary, and on this account would involve them all.

At midnight he was summoned before a council of the officers of the Inquisition, to hear and answer chargers against him. Before he was taken from his cell, he was loaded with chains, and his arms were pinioned behind him. If he had been the most dangerous and ferocious beast of the jungles of Bengal, he could not have been made more powerless from the actual fear of his judges. He was ushered into a dimly lighted room, where the President and the Judges of the Inquisition were assembled, consisting of thirteen, an ominous number for the prisoner or themselves, but which they thought for the prisoner. There was a profound silence like that of death, and a degree of fear and terror, but not on the part of Carabajal. He had comprehended the whole situation. He was convinced that he was simply about to be murdered by a band of conspirators under the form of Law and Religion and that he had only to wait his fate, as he was powerless. Alas! How many have been in the like situation, whose only crime was their merit or prosperity. He noticed every judge was draped in black and wore a masque, and every soldier present. What would have been his surprise to see these masques removed and find that the judges and the guards around them were some of his so-called best friends. This to him was a fatal indication. Carabajal looked around him fearlessly and said "What is the meaning of this insult and violence? If it is done from any false charges, I demand to hear them; if for the purpose of murdering me, I demand to see my wife and children," when there arose the Secretary of this tribunal, and read the following:

Don Louis de Carabajal Y Cueva, you have been charged and found guilty of the following crimes.

1st. Of being a Jew, and in the orgies and ceremonies of your Religion of having sacrificed and eaten a dozen Christian infants, subjects of our King.

2nd. Of having slain and destroyed many thousands of Indians, the loyal subjects of our King.

3rd. Of having robbed the loyal subjects of our King, by depriving them of the services of Indians as slaves or peons, and according them rights and privileges that only belong to Spaniards.

4th. Of taking from the care of the Holy Catholic Church, the education of the subjects of this Kingdom and establishing therein secular schools, where sciences are taught, unknown to the Church, and contrary to her Laws and doctrines.

The punishment of these crimes is death by fire, that the body, and if possible, the soul may be purified.

Carabajal listened with firmness and dignity. He now clearly perceived that their object was to murder him.

He replied that the Court had no authority or power to try him, that his patent as Royal Governor placed him beyond their jurisdiction.

As to being a Jew, the King knew him to be a Jew, when he appointed him, and that he was proud of this fact. "Does your Bible," said he, "not call them the chosen people of God? Have not my people given you both your religion and civilization—What is the difference between your civilization and the Roman? Is it not the elevation of womanhood? Who gave you the character of Rachael, Rebecca, and of Mary? Who and what were Christ, Peter, the founder of your church, Paul and all the other Apostles, but Jews? As to the sacrifice of Infants, this charge is beneath my contempt. You are the witnesses of the falsehood. In this charge I read your designs.

As to the destruction of Indians, it was in honorable war, and in your defence.

As to prohibiting their being made slaves of, I acknowledge it, with satisfaction.

As to establishing secular schools it was my legal right, under my patent.

Before you slay me, pause and reflect. It can only precede your own destruction a short time. The savages of the North will come here with fire and spear and not leave one of you alive, and of this building nothing but blackened walls.

As for me, I fear not death. No death or fire can touch my soul, and that is the ever-living part of me."

There was a Friar, Father Fransioli, an Italian who had been sent to Mexico by orders of the King, on account his great learning, and to keep up the Latin of the other Fathers. This Friar had occasional visions, on which occasions he was possessed; he now suddenly rose up with a corpse like face and glaring eyes, pointing his finger upward, as to the skies, and called out in a loud voice, "I see blood, blood. I see horse back riders dragging by their lassoes along the ground our brothers of this Inquisition. I see them torn by wild horses, limb from limb. I see this building a burning and smoking ruin. I see—" By this time some sturdy soldiers of the guard got control of the poor Father, and carried him out of the room, whilst his voice could still be heard shrieking, "I see blood, blood, blood."

The President then arose from his chair and said, "Don Louis de Carabajal Y Cueva, I sentence you after the finding of this Court of the Holy Inquisition, that you burn by fire, until you are dead, and that execution shall take place at 6 o'clock to-morrow morning."

Carabajal was about to protest that there had been no trial, in his presence, and against the illegality of the proceedings, when by the orders of the President he was hurried from the room.

Let no pious Catholics feel indignant nor the believers in other religions condemn the Catholic religion or the church. The Catholic religion had no more to do with this, than with thousands of other iniquities—murders and robberies perpetrated in the name of Religion—Liberty—Virtue or Country, by bad men, hypocrites and impostors.

The Non Catholic reader must not in his or her mind, hold the Catholic church, or the Pope responsible for these wrongs. These men were acting independent of the church, or the tenets inherent in the Catholic Faith. They were not doing their duty as religiose, but were influenced entirely by the Hidalgos, and were actuated by the worst of personal motives, to wit: —the robbing and the enslaving of the Indians. The virtuous Las Cases and other eminent Catholics reprobated all such proceedings, and complaints were constantly sent from Rome to Philip II, but Mexico and other South American States, were so far off, and so filled with greedy adventurers, that by the time the influence of the church reached them, that influence had become very weak, and was overpowered by secular corruption.

In vain Carabajal requested to see his family, and his supposed faithful secretary, Montemayer. He was not allowed writing materials, to make a will, or give directions, or information about the Government. There was but one desire—to hurry him out of existence, and if possible leave no mark behind.

Sleep he had none. There had not been time for the utter exhaustion of nature.

At 5.30 o'clock he was called and ushered in to a large hall where he was astonished to see his little family. At first he supposed that out of humanity they had been allowed to see him, but on a second glance he saw that they were all manacled. Even his lame son and aged mother. Then his son told him that they had all been sentenced to death, after some trial they knew nothing of. When Carabajal heard this, glancing from one to the other, he suddenly pressed his hand to his heart, and raising himself upward upon his feet, he fell backward stone dead. The fortitude and courage of Carabajal had been tried hundreds of times, and it was never found wanting, but the very life of the Jew lives and breathes in the love of his family, and when be looked upon his aged mother, the eyes of his dear wife, his innocent and decrepid [sic] son, and his sweet daughters and faithful sisters, and thought of their terrible fate, it was more than his noble nature could endure and then broke his mighty heart and he fell dead. Then the poor son raising his hand and voice showed the superiority of the soul over the body, uttered a malediction against the slayers of his father, and called upon all to have fortitude, for, said he "our father has gone to our God, the one and the true God, and in a few minutes we shall join him. It is no punishment, it is a happy journey." The particulars of this heart rending and terrible event we will pass by, but it is shown that the death of every one of the family was heroic. The dead body of Carabajal was also tied to a stake and burnt with them, perhaps to make sure of his death. Thus ended the noble life of a man devoted to the good of humanity. Has it been the first? Alas! Will it be the last?

This legend would be imperfect, did I not inform the reader of the sequel of this wickedness. There is an old saying that "the mills of the Gods grind slowly, but very fine." In this case they ground very rapidly.

At 8 o'clock the Council met, which was usually presided over by Carabajal. This time it was presided over by Montemayer, who was immediately made President, until another Governor should be appointed.

The following Laws were passed:

1st. That all the Indians should be considered slaves, and that all the grants of Carabajal to the Indians should be abrogated.

2nd. That all education should be in charge of the clergy.

3rd. That all Jews should he expelled from the Kingdom, because they were anti-Christ and interfered with the conversion of the Indians. (The real reason was of course to rob the Jews.)

4th. That the mines, lands, and territories should be divided up among the Spaniards, according to equity and justice. (This meant iniquity and injustice.)

They also decided to keep the fate of Carabajal and his family secret, for as many days as possible, until the armed forces of the Hidalgos were properly placed and to apply to the viceroy for additional armed forces, and also that Montemayer should be appointed Governor. After other work of minor importance they adjourned. That morning an ominous silence reigned over the city. People spoke in whispers, and in bated breath. The very animals appeared to be affected. A vague rumor of the crime that had taken place, existed. It struck terror in the minds of people. It was noticed that many people were silently leaving the City. In the afternoon the Indians disappeared, from the mines. In the night there were fires in different parts of the City, and even out in the Country. The morning after the crime, that is the day after, the Hidalgos found that nearly all the horses had been stolen, and had disappeared. There was hardly a horse left in the city. The women and children were there, but the male adult Indians had all disappeared. The Jews were also leaving. They simply gathered up their personal property, and traveled south to old Mexico, and yet the decree that had passed in Council, had not been made public, but the knowledge of it existed. The wicked and fiendish death of Carabajal became publicly talked about and also the decrees, but this talk was behind closed doors and in whispers. The Hidalgos were sorely perplexed, they had no horses to pursue the fugitives to the mountains, and they were afraid to turn their backs upon their homes for fear of fire. Montemayer could give no advice. The Council met, and in the face of the strange condition of things, of all the male Indians and all the horses having departed; they were perplexed. They turned to Montemayer as they had formerly turned to Carabajal, but they found they turned to a man who could give no orders, but rather asked for them. Finally they decided simply to wait, until the return of the courier that had been sent to the viceroy, asking for the appointment of Montemayer, in the place of Carabajal, and of the Spanish army, to more thoroughly enforce the decrees of council.

The fact is, both Jews and Indians for a long time had heard mysterious whisperings of the intentions of the Hidalgos, and their criticisms against their great leader, and silently as it were by common consent, they had decided in case of the murder of Carabajal, to steal away, the Jews to the south and the Indians to the north, with all the horses, to return soon as possible in company with the Yakos and Apaches, with fire and spear. Many of them had been warriors under Carabajal, and knew the use of firearms, and besides were skillful strategists. This was the cause of the wonderful change. Days passed on, and shops were not open, the mines were not worked, for want of men, and all business appeared to be suspended. The Spaniards armed themselves universally. In time a message arrived from the viceroy, with many congratulations, and a document appointing Montemayor Governor, and also with the information that an army was on the march, to take possession for the King, and to afford them protection. Montemayer instead of now rejoicing at the success of his schemes and treachery, when he held this document, felt as though it was worse than a poisonous scorpion in his hand. He already had realized how much easier it was to be a mere clerk than it was to govern, when possessed of no head for it. Now Spaniards commenced pouring in from the north with terrible news, the spies, formerly employed by Carabajal, did not come, but lame and wounded Spaniards, with tales as to how their families had been massacred, the houses burnt, and how it was rumored that cities had been destroyed. The Hidalgos fortified themselves behind entrenchments and awaited the arrival of the Spanish army. Finally it came, brave, weary and dust worn. Instead of seeing the beautiful city they had heard so much about, they saw what to them appeared to be a city of the dead, and many smoking ruins. They only tarried for a rest at Santa Lucia and Walnut Springs, and marched with the New Leon contingent to protect the cities farther north, which were said to be in danger. The Nueva Leon contingent should have been commanded by Montemayer as Governor, but he begged that the Spanish General would command, whilst he remained behind to forward supplies. Soon as the Spanish Army was out of sight he took refuge with the Holy Fathers, behind the stone walls of the Inquisition. When they looked upon his pale, sinister, and frightened face, they could only say, "Oh for a day of Carabajal." This action of Montemayer was to them the most frightful of omens.

The Spanish army was commanded by Don Juan Diaz de Vera, brave, and in European wars an efficient and successful Spanish general. Many of his men were veterans, and all of them, true to Spanish character, were brave. The discipline was wholly European. The Leon contingent was placed in advance, as better acquainted with the trails. As they were marching along, they passed several of the battle fields where Carabajal had won astounding victories. The selfish Hidalgos almost shed tears of grief when they thought of the past, and the gloomy present. They had none of that great confidence in themselves that they had when commanded by Carabajal. Their hearts also said, "Oh, for a day of Carabajal." The men were ordered to keep close ranks as possible, and the cavalry guarded the front and rear. The New Leon officers advised the old general to send cavalry in advance, and even begged to have it done, but the only reply was that, when he met the enemy, he would fight them, and that he would be responsible for the result. This system made the forage scarce and difficult, and the men suffered very much.

It was many days march north of Santa Lucia, when some Indian cavalry made their appearance, first in the advance then on the flanks and in the rear. This required a closer formation but such scarcity resulted, that they were compelled to forage wherever they had an opportunity, when the Indians would attack the foragers, and the Spaniards were constantly losing men and horses. So they continued their march until provision became very scarce, but all hoped for refreshment and reinforcement of men and horses when they got to the first city or colony in that region. When they got there they found nothing but a smoking mass of ruins. No beef, bread or horses were to be had and not a human being to be seen. A council of war was then held and it was decided that it was best to retreat, because if they continued on and the next city should be destroyed, which they reasonably believed to be the case, and no Indians should meet them in battle they would literally die of starvation. The retreat in the wilderness was a horrible affair. They commenced eating their horses. So long as these lasted, they at least had food, but they were rapidly disappearing. Now the Indians became bolder, and more numerous. Finally they came to a pass that was defended, and to their surprise a wall of rocks built across the trail, mounted with falconets. There opened a deadly fire upon the Spaniards, but the brave Spanish soldiers quickly charged it and captured the guns, when immense boulders of rocks were rolled down upon them from above. Many soldiers were killed, but orders were given to charge through the pass, which they did very bravely, and when they got to the open with considerable loss, they hardly saw an enemy.

The Spanish General thought this a strange sort of war. He began to comprehend the kind of enemy he had to fight, and it reminded him of the old Moorish tactics. But they marched on and finally the horses were all eaten, and men began to drop behind, when they would at once be murdered and scalped. They now numbered hardly half as many as they did when they marched out of the city of Mexico, with banners gay and to the sound of martial music. Day by day the army of Indians, as they became bolder, appeared to grow in numbers, and even ventured to attack, but the brave Spanish soldiers would give them a bloody reception and would feed upon the horses they killed. Still they pressed onward, slowly with their retreat.

One morning, just as the dawn began to light the Eastern sky, the sentinels at the outposts fired their arquebusses from all sides simultaneously, and dark masses of men on foot and mounted, with horrid noises, rushed upon the little army. The men were up and formed in a minute, and welcomed the attack with enthusiasm. They had been anxious for a battle, which had always been denied them, by the arts of the enemy, and this enemy, tired of the delay and encouraged by their depletion and weakness, could not supress their thirst for blood and revenge. They were received with a steady fire from muskets and falconets, and horses and riders fell in heaps around the little band, the brave Diaz de Vera with a choice band around him, rushed in every part of the field giving orders and fighting at the same time, now the prodigious energy and valor of these Spaniards shone in glory, and did honor to their conquering blood, but the more they killed, the more enemies appeared until they all realized that this was simply a fight to the death, as there was no retreat. The battle raged until there was no more Spaniards to die, not one attempted to seek safety in flight, and Diaz deVera died upon a heap of slain. The noon hour closed upon a field of death. The spoils of arms were immense, and welcome to the Indians. The ferocious Indians decorated their horses with scalps, and all pressed on to Santa Lucia to surprise the place if possible.

A few days after, they reached the city, they watered their almost spent horses at Walnut Springs, then rushed upon the place. The stupid inhabitants had not even retreated to the mountain tops which had formerly been fortified by Carabajal, but resting with implicit confidence in the supposed invincibility of the Spanish army, were completely exposed. Old men, women and children who were white were slaughtered without discrimination. A few of the leading people found shelter behind the stone walls of the Inquisition building. After the enemy had slaughtered and destroyed all that could be destroyed they quietly settled down around this last place of refuge until the remainder of the army, bringing artillery and gunpowder, should reach the place. Many of these were the old soldiers of Carabajal. This only required a day or two. A mine was soon sprung at one of the angles, when the Indians rushed in to renew the massacre. The thirteen Priests or Friars who had composed the Court of the Inquisition with Montemayor, had hid themselves in the torture chamber, but they were soon dragged out and instead of being killed upon the spot, were reserved for a worse fate.

The next day was set apart for rejoicing, before continuing the march to the south. The Indian women welcomed their husbands, who had saved them from slavery, and concubinage to their would be cruel task masters. A large level site, which now forms the beautiful Alameda of Monterey, was set apart for a fete. An immense circle was formed in imitation of a bull ring, into this there were brought the thirteen judges of the Inquisition, who were tied to thick posts driven into the ground. Under them was kindled a slow fire, and they were tortured in true Indian style until they died. It may well be supposed that they could now value the protection and services of Carabajal. After this the pale and trembling Montemayer was brought forth. He begged piteously for his life, but it was to ears of stone—life to him was sweet. His miserable mind could not look beyond it; his limbs were securely fastened by ropes to four wild horses in the same way that the Hidalgos had served the poor Yako. He was instantly torn limb from limb whilst the derisive shouts of joy and laughter were heard from thousands of Indians.

So ended for a time the power of the Spaniards, in Northern Mexico. A clean sweep of conquest and destruction was made and there was not a Spaniard left to tell the tale.

Years after this the Count of Monterey, viceroy of Mexico, collected an army and took possession of the site of Santa Lucia, and over its ruins arose in the language of a chronicle "The Metropolitan City of Monterey."

Appendix.

In the preparation of the above legend, tradition had to be mostly followed. The written accounts of the period of time relating to Carabajal are meagre and contradictory, as the injustice of the old Spanish Government, and the Inquisition were such that every possible effort was made not only to conceal the facts, but to destroy every particle of evidence. In turning over the leaves of some of the manuscripts of Carabajal, we will give a few extracts:

"A colony in order to be a success should not be conducted in a mere mercantile spirit of business, but more in a parental spirit, where the welfare of the colonist will be of the first consideration. If advantage is taken of the want of promptitude in complying with financial obligations, it would be destructive of the colony, for the simple reason, that as a rule colonists could never be found to be, what is called, business people, and by such a course, the whole colony would become panic stricken, and destroyed. So long as a colonist works and improves his land, to a reasonable extent, he should be allowed grace, with the certainty that he will meet all his obligations in the end. But dishonest advantage should not be allowed to be taken of this general principle. Certain rules should be formulated and adhered to, and they should be such rules as are certain to advance the material and moral welfare of the colony. These principles may be divided into the materialistic and the spiritualistic. The former consists of agricultural and manufacturing development which should always go together. The latter, the educational and the aesthetic. In the educational the practical or manual work should go hand in hand with the abstract or the theoretical. This makes learning easy, by constant illustration. The youthful mind is fond of the use of the hand, in concert with thought, and in this way never tires or forgets. Where the principles of agriculture and horticulture are taught in this way, they are never forgotten. The same of mechanics. The human mind in this way is aided and uplifted by manual labor, or assistance, but to expect that the youthful mind can grasp the abstract or theoretical without this aid, is to expect the impossible.

Free libraries should be established, in order that all who want intellectual instruction or amusement by the medium of books, should have them readily accessible. These instructions should be supplemented by lectures and intellectual entertainments. There should in public schools be taught dancing, calisthenics and music.

In the aesthetic, the love of the beautiful should be taught. It is one of the highest and most spirituelle [*sic*] principles that govern human nature, and cannot be ignored without producing evil effects.

This should be carefully considered in laying out a country. The land should be laid out in convenient roads which should be made to conform to the topography of the ground and laid out wide and spacious and planted in rows of beautiful trees of different varieties. Many of them flowering, such as can easily be procured in a tropical climate. This is not only for their beauty, which is very great, but in order to induce rains and to save the country from droughts. They also attract birds which are essential in the cultivation of fruits by destroying insect enemies. This should be further induced, by placing fountains at the intersections of many of the roads, always made ornamental by some fine allegorical statuary. This feature in a tropical country as well as a temperate climate, is not only beautiful, but a boon to the animal creation. Seats should be placed at intervals, under the most umbrageous trees, where the weary pedestrian can find rest and shade.

A society should be formed among the people for the propagation and preservation of these trees and also the cultivation of flowers. Of these the Mexican women are particularly fond, and the country soon becomes redolent and sweet with flowers, and musical with the hum of bees. Plans should be given out for small neat habitations suitable to the climate, and they should all be required to be set back a certain distance from the roadside, and thus afford room for flowers and shrubbery. In this space should often be seen the pretty fountain or statue. Thus beauty should be combined with usefulness and the surroundings of the people would be an inspiration of mental culture and elevation.

The founder should also interest himself constantly in the procuring of valuable seeds and plants from all parts of the world, suitable to the climate. But care should not stop here, the Founder, after the colony should get far enough to produce something to sell, in the way of agriculture and manufactures, should then pay personal attention to finding a market where they could be sold. Not only to find a market but to see that the inexperienced colonists should not fall into the hands of dishonest consigners or commission men, and in this way be robbed of their toil.

He should also lend his hand to rearing the Church or the Synagogue, for after all, man has to look Heavenward for consolation and hope."

THE END

The facts of the above legend were picked up during a two months sojourn in Monterey in the winter and spring of 1894.

C. K. L.

NOTES

A retired teacher of literature, film and writing on the high school and college levels, Vince Farinaccio is the author of *Nothing to Turn Off: The Films and Video of Bob Dylan* and the upcoming biography of Charles K. Landis, *Before the Wind*. He is a recipient of the Vineland Historical and Antiquarian Society's "Making the Difference" award for his dedication in preserving Vineland's history through his weekly column in *The Grapevine* newspaper. His articles have also appeared in the journals *The Bridge* and *Montague Street*.

Steve DeCicco, a graduate of the Literature Program of Stockton University, assisted in an earlier effort to republish "Carabajal," and current editors began work where he left off.

The punctuation within this text follows that printed in the first edition. The spelling of the original has largely been retained, although some obvious typographical errors have been silently corrected. The paragraphing has been modernized.

A Trip to Mars by Charles K. Landis (136 pages, paperback) is available for purchase from the Vineland Historical and Antiquarian Society or the South Jersey Culture & History Center. Copies are also available through Amazon.

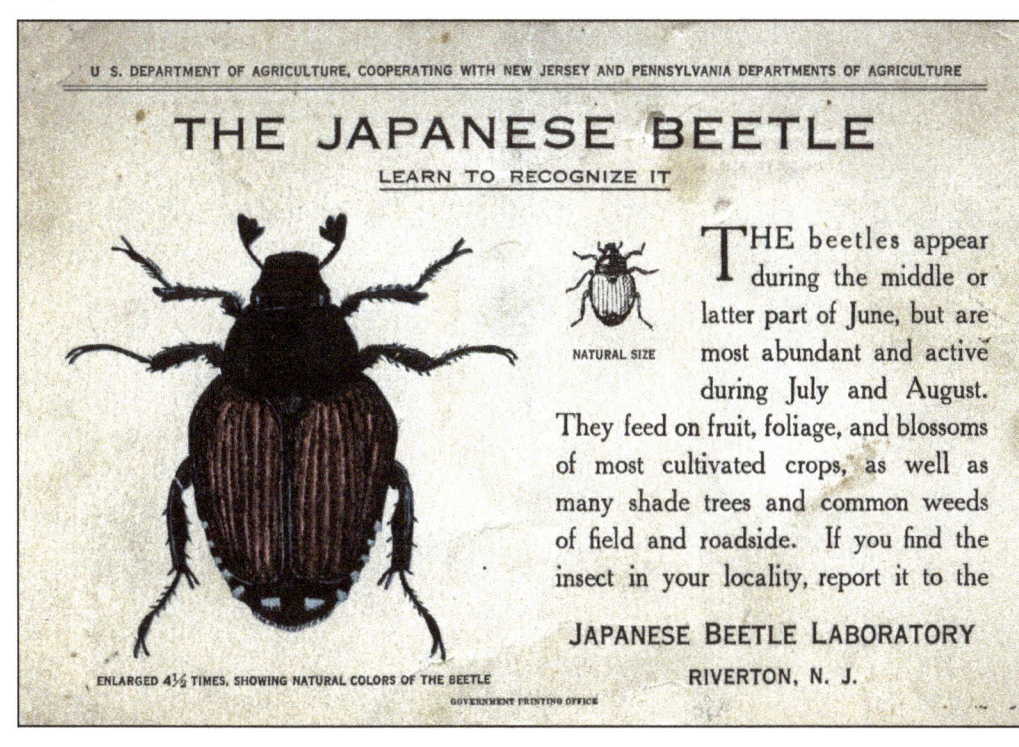

The Japanese Beetle. The Henry A. Dreer Company, which had its primary nursery in Riverton, Burlington County, New Jersey, imported Japanese iris bulbs circa 1916. The soil surrounding these bulbs apparently contained the larvae of Japanese beetles. The beetles matured and became the scourge of the United States, which labeled the beetle a most destructive insect. With no natural predators in America, the beetle ravaged gardens and farm fields spreading out from Riverton. The U.S. Department of Agriculture established a Japanese beetle laboratory in Riverton to study the insect and find methods to counteract its voracious appetite. To aid local residents in identifying and collecting specimens the laboratory mailed out these postcards.

Artistic interpretation of the Caldwell and Woodruff sawmill, Galloway Township, New Jersey, c. 1815, with the future Lake Fred in background.

Reimagining a Remnant of the Past at Stockton

Drawing by James Pullaro

History by Paul W. Schopp

The clattering wooden gear train and the resonant rhythmic "voopa, voopa, voopa" of the vertical saw blade slicing through the dogged log riding on the sawmill's shotgun carriage echoed through the surrounding pines and cedar swamps. It is 1815 and business partners James B. Caldwell and Elias D. Woodruff began operating their sawmill in the spring after constructing a dam and building the mill in January 1815. The illustration on the facing page by James Pullaro is an artistic rendering of how that sawmill might have appeared. The dam and mill stood on an 111-acre tract of land the business partners purchased from Samuel Whitall.[1] They actually acquired a total of six parcels of land in this $5000 transaction as tenants in common, including the 111-acre lot; they also purchased other lands for cutting timber. In the process of building their sawmill dam, Caldwell and Woodruff succeeded in creating the body of water known today as Lake Fred on Stockton University's Galloway campus.

In June 1819, the two men sold four of the six parcels of land acquired in 1815, including the 111-acre tract, to Nehemiah Blackman for $1850.[2] The deed contains no specific mention of the Caldwell and Woodruff milldam and sawmill, but the sale did include "all and singular the buildings, improvements...," etc.

The following year, the federal decennial census incorporated schedules for manufacturers, including sawmills. Nehemiah Blackman returned the questionnaire listing a gristmill and two sawmills. The gristmill and one sawmill stood in present-day Port Republic and the other sawmill was most likely the former Caldwell and Woodruff mill. While Blackman did not distinguish between his two sawmills, he provided the following information:

Whole quantity and kind of machinery: 2 saw mills, three saws, 4 water wheels & 2 ray wheels & 2 carriages [a ray wheel, operated by water, moved the log carriage forward through the saw blade]

The nature and names of the articles manufactured: By the saw mill: cedar boards, pine plank, boards & scantling.[3]

The mill appears as late as c.1860 on the Gloucester Town and Farm Association plat map, the so-called Bullinger map, but it does not appear on the 1872 F. W. Beers map of Atlantic County.[4,5] Eventually agriculturalists, including A. J. Rider, gained control of the lake and it served for many years as a cranberry bog.[6]

A half-mile downstream from the Caldwell and Woodruff sawmill, a mill complex almost 60-years older operated using the same waters of Morss Mill Branch (now denominated Moss Mill). Robert Morss, along with his friend and business partner, William Burnett, started cutting boards at their new sawmill in the fall of 1757. The new mill stood on a 50-acre tract of land first surveyed to Burnett in May of the same year, located about one mile up the Middle Run or Morss Mill Branch of Nacote Creek at present-day Swan Lake, Galloway Township.[7] Six years after constructing the new mill, Robert Morss sold his first sawmill, located in the settlement then known as Wrangleborough, to Elijah Clark in an unrecorded transaction.[8,9] Folklore suggests that Wrangleborough received its appellation from the frequent pugilistic exhibitions that once occurred there, but the word "wrangle," more properly spelled "wrangel,"

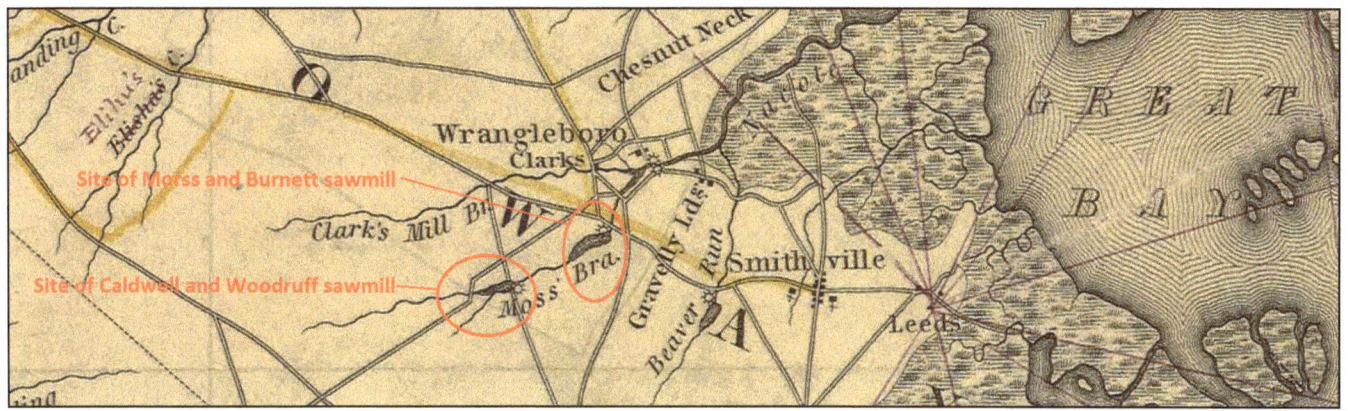

This detail from Thomas Gordon's *A Map of the State of New Jersey with Part of Adjoining States, Second Edition, Improved to 1833*, denotes the location of both sawmills described above, located near present-day Port Republic and the settlement of Smithville, Galloway Township, Atlantic County, New Jersey.

is a fourteenth-century Middle English word for the rib of a boat.[10] With the shipbuilding industry then flourishing along the Mullica River and elsewhere in the area, it makes sense that the sawyers residing in the hamlet of Wrangleborough specialized in producing ribs for the boat and shipyards dotting the waterways of West New Jersey.

In 1775, Robert Morss added a gristmill to his operations, constructing it at the opposite end of the dam from his sawmill.[11] Morss continued operating both mills with the aid of his two sons, Nehemiah and Jonas, and friend, William Burnett, until Robert's death in November 1789.[12] Dying intestate, i.e., without a will, the Gloucester County Orphans Court ordered the mills to be devised to Nehemiah and Jonas. Honoring a verbal agreement between their father and William Burnett, the two brothers conveyed a moiety or half-interest in the sawmill and other lands to Burnett.[13] The siblings and Burnett persisted in their operations at the mill complex until 1824, when John Marshall acquired the mills.[14] He continued logging operations into the 1850s. By 1862, an advertisement, shown below, for selling the property states that it comprises a house, a sawmill and about 58-acres of land. The sales notice states that "The Mill Pond is now drawn off, is large, and thought suitable for the cultivation of cranberries."[15]

PUBLIC SALE.
To be sold, at Public Vendue, on THE TWENTY-NINTH INST., at 2 o'clock, P. M., At the house of ELISHA HUDSON, MAY'S LANDING, ATLANTIC Co., N. J., A DWELLING HOUSE, SAW MILL, and about FIFTY-EIGHT ACRES OF LAND, (known as Marshall's Mill,) situate in Galloway Township, Atlantic County, N. J., one mile from Port Republic.
The Mill Pond is now drawn off, is large, and thought suitable for the cultivation of Cranberries.
Persons desirous of viewing the same, can call on JOB BALLINGER, near Leed's Point, or HENRY MARSHALL, on the premises.
The purchase money, except $500, can remain secured on the property by bond and mortgage.
SAML. NICHOLSON,
CHARLES L. WILLETS,
Assignees of Job Ballinger.
5th mo. 5th, 1862.-3t

West Jersey Press (Camden, NJ), May 21, 1862, 3.

Endnotes

James Pullaro is a Stockton graduate and current Stockton staff member. He grew up on the western edge of the Pine Barrens and now calls Leeds Point home. An ecstatic enthusiast of the New Jersey Pine Barrens, James has studied and explored the most remote tracts of the forest to discover her most well kept secrets. As an artist, James has recently set his sights on blending his love for history and ecology with his love for art and illustration.

Historian Paul W. Schopp, Assistant Director of the South Jersey Culture & History Center at Stockton University, has maintained a keen interest in the history of technology from the earliest days of his career. His published works involving technology include *Linseed Oil Mills in New Jersey 1732 – 1955* and *The Trail of the Blue Comet*.

1. Gloucester County Deed Book U, 420.
2. Gloucester County Deed Book EE, 9.
3. Records of the 1820 Census of Manufactures, Schedules for New Jersey. Microform edition. Washington, DC: National Archives and Records Administration.
   Although the invention of the circular saw blade occurred in the late eighteenth century, the long-standard vertical or up-and-down sawblades, either singular or ganged, continued to be used in most sawmills until the 1840s or so. By the late 1880s, blade manufacturers began producing large bandsaw style blades for use in sawmills, allowing these mills to increase production of lumber for a growing country. Scantling refers to thin strips of wood that crossed roof rafters at right angles and to which wood shingles were attached.
4. *Plan of the Lands of the Gloucester Farm and Town Association...*, Egg Harbor City, NJ: Gloucester Farm and Town Association, c.1860.
5. F. W. Beers, *Topographical Map of Atlantic Co. New Jersey*, New York City, NY: Beers, Comstock & Cline, 1872.
6. Clarence J. Hall, "Would Like to 'Kindle Fire Under New Jersey Industry,'" *Cranberries: The National Cranberry Magazine* (February 1946): 6-8.
7. West New Jersey Surveyor General's Record Book H, 227.
8. West New Jersey Surveyor General's Record Book U, 196. Trenton, NJ: New Jersey State Archives.
9. Gloucester County Deed Book N, p. 25. Woodbury, NJ: Gloucester County Clerk's Office.
10. *Oxford English Dictionary*, Volume W, 342.
11. West New Jersey Surveyor General's Record Book P, 127.
12. New Jersey Secretary of State Will Collection, Volume 30, 138. Trenton, NJ: New Jersey State Archives.
13. Gloucester County Deed Book M, 43-46.
14. Gloucester County Deed Book NN, 403.
15. "Public Sale." *West Jersey Press* (Camden, NJ), May 21, 1862, 3. Microform edition.

Call for Articles

The South Jersey Culture & History Center at Stockton University publishes twice-yearly issues of *SoJourn*. We actively seek community members, avocational historians, and scholars to contribute essays on topics related to South Jersey. Illustrations to accompany these articles will be a plus. Articles should be written for laypersons who are interested and curious about South Jersey topics, but do not necessarily have expertise in the areas covered. Potential authors should check SJCHC's website for a link to a simplified style sheet guide for article preparation—https://blogs.stockton.edu/sjchc/—or just follow the style in this issue. Journal editors will be happy to guide any would-be authors. In certain instances, Stockton editing interns may be assigned to help research topics and/or assist authors with writing.

Sample topics might include:
Biographical sketches of important but forgotten local people; the development or succession of a community's roads, bridges or buildings; local transportation (focused by mode, area or era) and what changes it wrought in the served communities; history of community businesses and industries (wineries, garment factories, agriculture, boat building, clamming, etc.); old school houses, old hotels, or meeting halls; narrative descriptions of local geographical features; essays concerned with folklore, music, arts; and reviews of new local interest publications. Photo essays and old photograph and postcard reproductions are welcome with applicable captions. In short, if a South Jersey topic interests you, it will likely interest *SoJourn*'s readers.

Parameters for submissions:
• Submissions must pertain to topics bounded within the 8 southernmost counties of New Jersey (Burlington & Ocean Counties and south)
• Manuscripts should be approximately 3,000 – 4,000 words long (5 to 7 pages of single-spaced text and 9 to 12 pages including images)
• Manuscripts should conform to the *SoJourn* style sheet, available here: https://blogs.stockton.edu/sjchc/sojourn-style-sheet/
• Manuscripts, if at all possible, should be submitted in digital format (Word- or pdf-formatted documents preferred)
• Images should be submitted as high-resolution tiff- or jpeg-formatted files (editors can assist with digital conversion of photos if necessary)
• Complete and appropriate citations printed as endnotes should be employed (see style sheet)
• Original submissions only. Copyright licenses for all images must be obtained by the author or should be copyright-free figures and/or figures in the public domain
• If essays are accepted, authors should submit a short 50 to 100 word autobiographical statement
• Articles need to be more than just a chronology of the given topic. The author should be able to properly contextualize the subject by answering such questions as: a) why is this important?; b) what is the impact on the local or regional history? and c) how does it compare to similar events/personages/changes/processes in other localities?

Call for submissions:
Submissions for fall issues are due before September 1; for spring issues, January 15.
Send inquiries or submissions to Thomas.Kinsella@stockton.edu.

Appeal to the Community:
Emma Van Sant Moore (1877 – 1965: of New Gretna, Hammonton, and Millville) corresponded with A. Hollis Koster in the 1940s and 1950s, primarily about poetry and South Jersey folklore. The Bjork Library at Stockton University has received a donation of Van Sant Moore's letters from this correspondence; the whereabouts of Koster's side of the correspondence, if extant, is unknown. SJCHC is planning a study of Van Sant Moore's letters and poetry. We hope that any relatives, friends, or community members who may have memories of Mrs. Moore, or letters from her or from Koster, or others, will contact SJCHC. Any such materials will surely enrich the study.

www.ingramcontent.com/pod-product-compliance
Lightning Source LLC
Chambersburg PA
CBHW050258090426
42734CB00026B/3496